Human Rights

In ever loving memory of S.M. Fagan

Human Rights

Confronting Myths and Misunderstandings

Andrew Fagan

Deputy Director, Human Rights Centre, University of Esssex, UK

Edward Elgar
Cheltenham, UK • Northampton, MA, USA

Published by
Edward Elgar Publishing Limited
The Lypiatts
15 Lansdown Road
Cheltenham
Glos GL50 2JA
UK

Edward Elgar Publishing, Inc.
William Pratt House
9 Dewey Court
Northampton
Massachusetts 01060
USA

Paperback edition 2011

A catalogue record for this book
is available from the British Library

Library of Congress Control Number: 2009930853

MIX
Paper from
responsible sources
FSC
www.fsc.org   FSC® C018575

ISBN 978 1 84844 161 3 (cased)
ISBN 978 1 84980 982 5 (paperback)

Typeset by Cambrian Typesetters, Camberley, Surrey
Printed and bound by MPG Books Group, UK

Contents

Acknowledgements

I have had the privilege and the sheer good fortune to have spent the last ten years teaching human rights at one of the most intellectually enriching environments in the world for this subject: the University of Essex. My understanding of human rights has benefited greatly from many of my colleagues there. Foremost among these are Kevin Boyle, Will Cartwright, Tom Cornford, Janet Dine, Michael Freeman, Paul Hunt, Todd Landman, Sheldon Leader, Noam Lubell, Damien Short and Tom Sorell. I must also acknowledge the lasting influence of J.M. Bernstein, Barry Clarke and Simon Cohn, all of whom inspired me on the development of my academic life in their different ways. My approach to human rights and appreciation for the practice of human rights have been significantly influenced by the many hundreds of undergraduate and postgraduate students I have taught over the last decade. Their commitment to the subject has consistently served to remind me that human rights is not just another academic subject: the effects of our teaching extend far beyond the relatively secure realm of academia and engage with a world still far too beset by injustice and suffering. Occasionally, we academics need to be reminded of this, and my students at Essex have never failed to do so. I am deeply grateful to them for that. There are too many to identify individually but the following deserve a mention: Sarah Ellis, Claudia Bonny Farray, Rhiannon Morgan, Justin Pettit, Maria Furstenau Rodrigues and George Wright. Finally, to the two principal women in my life: Julia and Claudia, I owe an inexpressible debt of gratitude for their love and understanding.

Andrew Fagan
University of Essex
January 2009

Introduction

This book, as the sub-title indicates, aims to confront a number of enduring and significant myths and misunderstandings which afflict both the theory and the practice of human rights. Many other academic human rights books approach the subject by means of a conventional classificatory structure which distinguishes between such things as the different categories of human rights, enduring themes and concepts within the subject-matter and established issues in the application of human rights to the 'real world'. Many of these works have made a vitally important contribution to the understanding of human rights amongst students and practitioners alike. The extent of their success can be gauged by the relatively little that remains to be usefully written within this genre. In an effort to avoid mere repetition, I have opted for a different approach to the subject. Human rights have become, in many parts of the world, a household term. In some parts of the world, human rights have become a veritable totem around which campaigns for social justice and against oppression have taken root. An awareness of and an appeal to human rights have spread beyond the realm of elite political and intellectual communities and have come to exert a profound influence upon many people's political, economic and social projects and aspirations. It would be wrong, or at least deeply egocentric, to claim that we, that is everyone, now live in a veritable age of human rights. This is, if you will, the foremost myth in need of correction. After all, the ultimate criterion for determining whether we live in such an age is the extent to which all people everywhere can be said genuinely to possess and exercise their fundamental human rights. This age has yet to arrive, as evidenced by the countless millions, if not billions, of human beings whose basic human rights are systematically denied every waking day of their lives. Like many other so-called historical 'ages' or epochs before, the age of human rights remains a relatively rarefied property of the privileged few, who are sometimes too quick to misconstrue their own conditions for those of others. A commitment to human rights entails, however, a commitment to satisfactorily securing the conditions required for a world finally free from the effects of systematic misery and avoidable suffering. Only then can we genuinely declare ourselves to be the bearers of an age of human rights. In recent years, despite a number of deeply significant geo-political developments and ever-expanding global wealth, there have emerged a number of challenges to human rights claims to normative hegemony. These have come from various quarters and have taken various forms. The principal aim of this book is to explore and respond to a selection of these challenges, which I have labelled, uncharitably perhaps to some, myths and misunderstandings.

The basis and the legitimate parameters of human rights cannot be excluded from critical analysis and scrutiny. To this extent, human rights are no different from any other potential subject of intellectual inquiry. I do not, therefore, consider all challenges to human rights as being merely wrong in a moral or an epistemological sense. However, a significant proportion of the intellectual 'friction' within the theory and practice of human rights needs to be confronted with slightly less intellectual tolerance than is appropriate for other forms of deliberative dispute and disagreement. A commitment to human rights is not equivalent to a preference for a particular art-work or a consumer commodity. Human rights, in so many ways, affect the very capacity and opportunity to engage in deliberation and differences of opinion in the first place. They are, in this sense, truly foundational. This does not absolve human rights from any and all criticism, but we need to remind those who challenge the basis and moral authority of human rights that they can do so only to the extent that their own human rights are not unduly restricted and denied in these respects. To amend von Neurath's familiar metaphor a little, we cannot dismantle the lifeboat our very existence is largely dependent upon so long as we remain on open and tempestuous seas.

Myths differ from mere misunderstandings in some important respects. Without resorting to the Oxford English Dictionary, I take myth to possess a decidedly and all-important intentional quality. Myths are deliberately created by some agent or collective body of agents with the aim of achieving some purpose or end through representing reality in a particular way. The reality represented is 'mythical' to the extent that it can be shown to be objectively 'false', partial or inaccurate. Misunderstandings can also be shown to be false or based upon erroneous reasoning, but lack the more overtly purposive and intentional quality of myths. The origins and motives of misunderstandings are typically far more random than their mythical counterparts. However, the ultimate distinction between the two is not completely cut and dried and, like many other discursive phenomena in these non-binary times, is better understood as marking opposing, idealised points on a spectrum. Having said that, it is useful to distinguish between the two in respect of human rights to the extent that it enables one to distinguish between the depth and potential intractability of the notion in question: misunderstandings are more easily overcome than more entrenched myths to the extent that the latter have more purposive 'weight' behind them. I draw the distinction in order to support the broader normative ambition of this work.

The scope of the ensuing discussion is intended to provide a sufficiently comprehensive and detailed engagement with human rights to enable a reader relatively new to the academic literature to gain a solid understanding and knowledge of the principal landmarks in this field. It is, however, necessarily limited and is not intended to address all of the most important aspects of understanding human rights in the current age. The content of this book is selective and some readers may lament the omission of their own particular areas of interest. I apologise for that. However, what is covered here aims to encourage all students and practitioners of human rights to reflect upon what they consider the basis and scope of human rights rightfully to be. To that extent, I have chosen to include myths and misunderstandings from across a wide range of specific positions within the academic human rights field. While some of the specific myths and misunderstandings considered have been chosen precisely because of their scepticism of or hostility to the doctrine, others have been chosen that are actually fully affirmative of the doctrine. I have chosen these because and only to the extent that their particular claims can be shown to be ultimately harmful to the moral authority and legitimacy of the doctrine: they ask for too much in the name of human rights and seek to extend human rights claims to areas of life where they do not apply.

Chapter 1 begins with an analysis of a misunderstanding and addresses an established tendency to confuse social privileges with human rights. I argue that this tendency has its roots within human rights theory and the difficulty in determining the basis and scope of what it means to be human in the first place. After considering the two dominant theoretical approaches to justifying human rights I propose an understanding which aims to restrict the application of human rights to essential conditions of human well-being.

Chapter 2 takes aim at a myth and engages with human rights as a distinct moral doctrine. The myth in question is that which views human rights in strictly legal terms and claims that human rights can only be said to legitimately exist as legal entities. Legal-positivism has had a profound effect upon the development of jurisprudence and has figured prominently in the critical literature upon human rights. My criticisms of these arguments offer nothing new to the debate but aim to remind us of the necessary persistence of the distinctly moral dimension of human rights, which is not reducible to, or dependent upon, legal recognition and codification.

Chapter 3 extends the argument of Chapter 2 to address the myth of human rights as a universally valid moral doctrine. This may appear, as stated, to be a simple contradiction on my part. Typically, refutations of legal-positivism have rested upon an appeal to moral universalism and a characterisation of legal-positivism as a form of moral relativism. This is correct. However, many, but not all, of the arguments presented in favour of human rights' universal validity have failed to engage with, or even acknowledge, the social basis to human rights. Continuing to insist or imply that human rights can be defended without engaging in analysis of the social conditions which have influenced them is intellectually naïve. It has also consistently run the risk of being criticised as a form of Eurocentricism. This chapter argues that successfully extending human rights' legitimacy requires a serious engagement with society and culture and aims to develop an argument which goes beyond merely repeating the mantra that culture and society have no bearing upon globally acceptable justifications of human rights.

Chapter 4 shifts focus to the relationship between human rights principles and nation-states. There is an established misunderstanding of human rights as a doctrine which is ultimately incompatible with the modern state. The origins of this view lie, to some degree, in a latent form of cosmopolitanism which, on some readings, accords little constructive role to the state in initiating or instituting a global morality. The singular role of the state as an abuser of human rights has also reinforced this view. I argue that a correct understanding of human rights as a contemporary moral doctrine must include a comprehensive and accurate account of the institutional capacity of the state to protect and promote human rights. As the world is presently structured, human rights cannot be achieved without utilising state power and resources.

Chapter 5 retains this focus by challenging an important myth concerning the relationship between democracy and human rights. An argument supportive of the state's role in upholding human rights requires a determination of what kind of state is best suited to this end. The conventional response to this question identifies democracy as both necessary and sufficient to this end. However, democracy is a concept with many interpretations. One in particular has detrimentally affected the exercise of human rights, to the extent that it has been argued that democracy is based upon the enjoyment of civil and political rights and does not require any significant concern for their economic, social and cultural counterparts. I present an established argument against this particular myth which draws upon Henry Shue's notion of rights holism.

Extending the notion of rights holism to another area of human rights concern, Chapter 6 proceeds to focus upon a significant misunderstanding concerning the relationship between rights and duties. I place this analysis in the context of a discussion of economic justice. Many have argued that human rights are insensitive to duties. Various explanations have been offered in support of this claim. For example, it is frequently argued that human rights are unduly influenced by moral egoism and the consolidation of self-interest. Something resembling this view is undeniably discernible in some accounts of human rights. However, I shall argue that these accounts are false to the extent that they fail adequately to conceptualise the necessary role of duty as a counterpart to the possession and effective exercise of any human right. If one takes seriously the view that rights are correlative with duties, one must draw a different conclusion from that which reduces the notion of duty to the status of a mere afterthought.

Chapter 7 concludes my discussion by bringing together all of the various strands and elements of the previous chapters. The purpose of this final chapter is to outline a positive and constructive vision and account of human rights in the contemporary age. This aims to transcend the more overtly negative purpose of demonstrating the errors and weaknesses of other approaches to specific aspects of human rights. My ambition is not thereby to end all subsequent discussion of the subject at this level, but rather to present an account which suffers less from those myths and misunderstandings which affect both our understanding of human rights and, more importantly, the prospects for their realisation. I leave it to individual readers to decide how successful I have been in this regard.

1. The basis and scope of human rights

INTRODUCTION

Chapter 1 delineates the basis and scope of human rights through the analysis of a misunderstanding. More often assumed than stated, this misunderstanding attributes too much to human rights as a consequence of perceiving the doctrine as a fully comprehensive morality for human life. This misunderstanding serves to blur the important distinction between human rights and social privileges; that is to say goods which are essential to human life and agency and those which may be objects of desire for some but are certainly not constitutive of human agency *per se*.

Misconceiving the basis and the legitimate scope of human rights has, at times, undermined the doctrine's legitimacy in the eyes of some. The human rights 'inflationism' which typically accompanies this misunderstanding is damaging to the doctrine in multiple ways. Thus, it runs the very real risk of trivialising human rights demands by over-extending their scope to cover what are widely considered to be mere social privileges. Similarly, it obscures the all-important issue of desert in the enjoyment of human rights, in so far as privileges are typically understood as entailing some reward process, which is absent from the grounds for possessing a human right. Most importantly of all, it serves to obscure the moral imperative for human rights and the very point of their existence in the first place. This chapter focuses, then, primarily upon the distinction between human rights and social privileges. This entails a return to a consideration of *the* two foundational questions of human rights: what is their purpose and why should they exist? I address these questions by analysing two different philosophical theories of human rights: the interest theory and the choice theory approaches. Ultimately, both of these approaches argue that the purpose of human rights and the justification for their existence lie in the essential contribution they make to human agency: both approaches present human rights as veritably constitutive attributes of human agency. I criticise this approach. Human rights exist not to ensure human life *per se* but to protect and promote the conditions for a certain quality of life for all. In this respect, human rights are inherently normative. Understanding the purpose and justification of human rights in this way raises questions over the proper scope of their application and at what level the quality of life criterion can justifiably be set. I conclude this chapter with a discussion of this vitally important consideration.

METHADONE AND THE HOLOCAUST

What is the ultimate purpose of human rights? The modern human rights movement emerges out of a response to the Holocaust, that 'hideous icon of human suffering for post-war generations' (Fagan, 2008: 94). The Universal Declaration of Human Rights was certainly motivated, in part, by an attempt to place effective restrictions upon any state's ability systematically to annihilate whole populations. The response to the Holocaust and genocide marks the spot at which the modern human rights movement established an institutional foothold in the new world order which emerged after the end of the Second World War. No sane human being could possibly question the legitimacy and moral authority of human rights as a means for seeking to ensure that the very worst excesses of inhumanity would not be repeated. Contrast this with some more recent claims to human rights. In the UK in April 2008 a class-action case was successfully brought against the British government by 200 prisoners who claimed that the Prison Service violated their human rights through failing to provide them with a methadone substitute for their heroin addiction.[1] Inevitably this was reported as securing a human right to receive drugs paid for by UK taxpayers. Subsequent press reporting presented this as yet another absurd violation of common sense in the name of human rights. Protestations by civil liberty organisations and some medical professionals fell on mostly deaf ears. Popular opinion and the media should not be the ultimate arbiters of what human rights entitle anyone to. However, it would be foolish to deny that the scope of the application of human rights, from protection against genocide to a right to methadone, serves to raise very serious questions about the conditions under which human rights claims may legitimately be made. The scope of human rights obviously extends beyond seeking to protect populations from genocide, but how much further does it extend?

The misunderstanding of human rights this chapter focuses upon owes its existence to a complex relationship between the basis and the scope of human rights. There has been a tendency amongst some theorists of human rights to treat questions concerning the basis and the scope of human rights as separate, though related, concerns. In this way, one may identify that which grounds anyone's claim to possess human rights, before proceeding to delineate how far this claim extends and which human goods should be identified as human

---

[1] See 'Inmates Win Cold Turkey Pay-out', *The Times*, 18 April 2008.

rights. Thus, Jack Donnelly combines an answer to the basis and scope questions when he writes that human rights 'are the rights one has because one is
a human' (2002: 7). Donnelly's statement is certainly clear, concise and
unequivocal concerning the basis of human rights but it fails to provide criteria for adequately addressing the scope dimension contained within his formulation. All human beings may legitimately claim human rights. This is
fundamental, but not sufficient for the purposes of determining which aspects
of human life and action should be identified as belonging to the category of
human rights. One might be inclined to suggest that all those elements which
make anyone 'human' can be legitimately identified as enjoying the status of
human rights. On this view, human rights are instruments for being human in
the first place. The purpose of human rights and the ultimate justification for
their existence consist in their status as prerequisites for human agency. This
is the approach which the vast majority of theorists of human rights take in
their attempts to address the foundational questions. On this view, a human
right to protection from genocide is obviously legitimate, whereas a human
right to manage an addiction, on the face of it, is somewhat less indubitable.
The one seems an unequivocal human right whereas the other appears to some
just as unequivocally as a social privilege to which the beneficiaries are not
entitled. The basis and the scope of human rights are closely, if not inextrica-
bly, related and consist of their necessity for being human in the first place.
We have human rights because we are human, and they legitimately exist
because they are a prerequisite for anyone being human in the first instance.
This formulation is unmistakably tautological. It is surprising, therefore, to see
just how central it is for many attempts to justify human rights and provide
criteria for determining the legitimate scope of human rights and thereby
providing for the separation of human rights from social privileges.

BEING HUMAN AND CLAIMING HUMAN RIGHTS: INTEREST THEORY APPROACH

It is impossible to begin to engage with the foundational questions of human
rights without delving into the theoretical terrain of the nature of being human.
Typically, attempts to answer these questions and thereby provide a justification for human rights as a distinct moral doctrine seek to identify the fundamental elements or prerequisites for human agency. Theoretical justifications
of human rights invariably begin and end with an attempt to identify what it is
that ultimately constitutes us as human agents. All such attempts aim to identify what we all commonly share by virtue of being human and then construct
from this commonality an account of the scope and application of human
rights.

The specific subject-area of attempts to justify human rights tends to be dominated by philosophy. Despite contemporary philosophy's reluctance to engage with questions concerning a purported essence or first nature of humankind, the tradition of attempting to define and identify first principles and foundational conditions retains some adherents within philosophy, and some of these have turned their attention towards human rights as an appropriate domain for this type of exercise. Philosophy, though, does not enjoy a complete monopoly in this field as others have also sought to contribute justifications for human rights through the identification of some purported human essence. Different approaches to the same goal do exist but do not divide along academic disciplinary lines alone. The more appropriate distinction is that between interest theory and choice theory approaches to justifying human rights.[2] Interest theory provides the focus of this section and choice theory will be analysed in the following section.

The *interest theory* approach is a label applied to a number of theorists whose separate attempts to identify the basis and scope of human rights contain some significant similarities and differences. I shall discuss both in turn, beginning with the similarities. The label has been applied to the work of John Finnis, Bryan Turner, Martha Nussbaum and Amartya Sen, amongst others. The common basis for the interest theory approach consists of the appeal each theorist makes to the existence of fundamental human interests. Human beings are viewed as physiological and social agents who require the sufficient protection and promotion of certain interests in order to be human. These interests pre-exist, so to speak, the institution of human rights and social institutions more generally. That is to say, human rights are viewed as grounded in our very nature and exist in order to promote and protect those interests which constitute us: human rights are viewed as the mechanism through which these interests are best identified and secured. Historically and analytically, the concept of human interests precedes that of human rights. However, it would also be accurate to say that the language of human rights is fast replacing and superseding that of human interests, to the extent that the two are viewed in many quarters as simply synonymous. This can be unfortunate to the extent that it may obscure how some interest theorists conceive of human rights: as instrumental means for securing those 'goods' and interests which (purportedly) make us what we are. On this view, human rights are considered to be instrumentally valuable to realising our fundamental interests, rather than the form those interests must necessarily take.

---

[2] The philosopher Bernard Williams (1985) argued that all moralities can ultimately be labelled as either interest or choice theories. The distinction is sometimes drawn between interest and *will* theories. I consider will and choice to be synonymous, but, like Williams, prefer the latter term.

Few interest theories foreground the concept of human nature in their formulations of the basis and scope of human rights, which is understandable, given the deeply controversial character of any such appeal. Many theorists for example, have rejected the very notion of some essence or first nature to humankind. Over the past fifty years or so, the discussion of what our nature may be has been completely transformed by the contributions of historians, social anthropologists and sociologists who have empirically challenged a conception of human 'nature' as timeless and unchanging. Appeals to human nature or essential human interests have increasingly provoked disagreement and dissensus, rather than agreement and consensus. This is also apparent within the interest theory approach, insofar as different interest theorists present different accounts of our fundamental interests.

Drawing upon a tradition of natural law, John Finnis (1980) argues that there are seven basic forms of human flourishing, which are universal and encompass social and physical attributes of the human condition, ranging from a capacity for practical reason, to play and recreation, culminating in a capacity for spiritual experience. He argues that this account is not beholden to some overly physiological conception of human nature and is comprehensive and robust enough to encompass the empirical diversity of human life. According to Finnis the function of human rights is to secure our access to and enjoyment of these seven basic forms of human flourishing and they are justified to the extent that they are successful in providing for this end. By contrast, the neo-Aristotelian philosopher Martha Nussbaum (2002) identifies ten basic goods, ranging from 'life', bodily health and bodily integrity to emotions, affiliation, which comprises friendship and respect, and finally, control over one's environment. Some may be inclined to dismiss the differences between Finnis and Nussbaum as mostly irrelevant to the underlying vision of humankind they seek to express. However, the differences are apparent enough and reveal the extent to which the two authors are influenced by different normative principles; visions of what humankind ought to be, rather than what it is. In this respect, they do share a somewhat 'idealised' account of humanity, which largely excludes human beings' capacity for inhumanity. It seems somewhat counter-intuitive to suggest that each and every one of us has a fundamental interest in our capacity for inhumanity, but perfectly reasonable to insist that an account of human rights takes this capacity into account. This line of reasoning raises a deeper issue for any attempt to justify human rights. After all, as I stated earlier, the modern human rights movement was motivated by the need to prevent the grossest forms of inhumanity. While the vision of humanity implied within the Universal Declaration of Human Rights (UDHR) owes much to the emancipatory and celebratory spirit of the Enlightenment, the Holocaust and not the Enlightenment underlies the drafting of the UDHR.

This raises what we may term the motivational question. The motivational question aims to account for why each and every human being has a fundamental interest in respecting human rights as a general institution. This is not a question for interest theories alone, and it will recur through different parts of this work. However, for the moment, it is important to see that different interest theories have dealt with this question in different ways. Both Finnis and Nussbaum imply that this question can be answered adequately by an accurate understanding of our nature and of human reason as a constituent of that nature: the realisation of our common attributes will entail the establishment of an institutional commonality. However, both Finnis and Nussbaum fail adequately to address those less worthy and salubrious aspects of our condition. One might say that both accounts fail to accord sufficient weight to the Holocaust and genocide as a human fact: both neglect the phenomenon of systematically induced human suffering as an essential feature of any account of humankind and correlative rights.

The same cannot be said of another interest theorist, the sociologist Bryan Turner. Like other interest theorists, Turner (2002) ultimately appeals to central features of the human condition as providing the basis and scope for the social institution of human rights. Unlike some other sociological contributions to the study of human rights however, Turner's contribution does attempt to identify some mostly asocial and trans-historical elements of the human condition out of which and in response to which our concern for human rights should be directed. Put succinctly, Turner argues that the institution of human rights exists to protect human beings from one another, as much as to provide for a more flourishing human life. The ultimate feature of the human condition, Turner argues, is that we are physically frail and potentially vulnerable to one another. Turner insists that this is a universal condition; by virtue of being physically embodied beings we are frail and vulnerable to one another. The function of human rights is to provide protection and security for all of us to a broadly equal degree. All must return to dust eventually, but in the meantime we all have a similar capacity for suffering. To the extent that this suffering has man-made causes, we all have an interest in avoiding and preventing human suffering as much as possible. Human rights aim not at achieving some perfect humanistic utopia but rather are motivated by our physical and social frailty and a desire to avoid or reduce our exposure to this.

How might the interest theory approach be criticised? Its most apparent weakness would appear to lie in the necessary role played by the concept of human nature as the foundation for purportedly essential interests. Placing to one side those who challenge the very notion of a human essence, it is clear that even those who do appeal to human nature harbour different conceptions of what our nature consists of. All accounts of human nature appear to be unduly partial and insufficiently comprehensive to provide a fully objective and accurate menu of essential human interests. Personally, I do not think this is the most important criticism of the interest theory approach. It would be foolish to deny that our physiological and social functioning is adversely affected by a lack of access to certain goods or attributes. The most obvious of these are, perhaps, food and water. I do not personally think that the identification of certain fundamental human interests, that is interests which positively promote our individual well-being, is an exercise doomed to failure. Interest theories should be commended precisely to the extent that they do place the fact of our embodiment at the very centre of any attempt to define the basis and scope of human rights. However, the interest theory approach suffers from at least one fundamental weakness, and this consists of what I earlier referred to as the motivational question.

Human rights address humankind but are ultimately possessed by separate individuals: individual moral sovereignty is central to the human rights doctrine.[3] Thus, in identifying the human rights which any individual may legitimately possess, we would appear to be bound to apply these to all human agents. Such neat conclusions can be easily drawn in the comfort of a theorist's study; in the real world however, things are rather different. Put bluntly, it is easier to see why I should take a self-interested reason in having my human rights secured than why I should simultaneously act to ensure that some distant other's human rights should also be secured. This would not matter if my actions and inactions had no bearing at all upon others' conditions. Unfortunately, however, they do. The unequal distribution of essential resources across the globe is an obvious case in point. Human rights exist against the backdrop of haves and have-nots where the immediate self-interest of the former may positively require the continuing deprivation of the latter.[4] This has critical consequences for the interest theory approach, which can be illustrated by critically analysing Turner's argument.

Turner has been criticised on many grounds, including for not being sufficiently 'sociological' in his approach to human rights (Waters, 1996). This claim harbours a number of rather different issues and concerns, but one of these is particularly important for present purposes. One may discern a distinct Hobbesian influence upon Turner's approach to human rights, grounded, as it is, upon our capacity to harm one another. Hobbes famously sought to identify a political means by which self-interested individuals might nevertheless prudentially live under the same political roof. While few go so far as to endorse his account of the Leviathan as the ultimate guarantor of prudential self-interest, his approach has profoundly influenced modern political theo-

---

[3]   I discuss moral sovereignty in greater detail in Chapter 2.

[4]   Explaining and defending this claim will constitute a principal element of Chapter 6.

rists who have similarly appealed to prudential self-interest as the basis for securing reciprocal respect for fundamental human rights (Gauthier, 1986).

For some drawing a comparison between Turner and Hobbes will serve to reinforce the validity of the former's claims. However, Turner's argument shares with Hobbes' (and other such theorists') a fundamental weakness. The weakness is, I believe, of a more empirical than purely normative character. I term this weakness a false political economy of harm. What do I mean by this? Like all contractarian accounts of the basis and scope of political authority, Turner's is vulnerable to an empirical falsification of one of his argument's central assumptions; namely, that all of these agents addressed by the theory are in fact similarly situated in respect of their capacity to harm or aid one another, or can be hypothetically represented as so situated. Turner's approach shares with other interest-theory-based accounts of human rights a desire to avoid appealing to unduly hypothetical or metaphysical visions of the nature of humankind and aims to restrict the vision to that which is empirically demonstrable or credible. Put simply, his account assumes the existence of a relatively level playing field, inhabited by each and every frail and vulnerable human being. This assumption is manifestly false, and its falsity has devastating effects upon his claims concerning each agent's motives for respecting others' human rights.

This criticism applies, of course, even within the nation-state context of much contemporary political theory. However, the theory of human rights must necessarily extend its boundaries well beyond national frontiers to embrace humankind in its entirety. When viewed from this perspective, the criticism is even more damning. It simply is not true to claim that the peoples of the world are similarly or equally vulnerable to one another. The so-called 'South', for example, has been far more vulnerable to the economic and political conditions of the 'North' than the other way round. We may be increasingly occupying a single global space, but the distribution of a capacity for harming others is anything but equal. This is important insofar as it potentially undermines a motivation for the relatively invulnerable peoples of the world to recognise the human rights of the vulnerable. A more 'rational' approach might be to erect barriers and secure borders, literally and figuratively, between communities: the establishment of so-called 'gated communities' on a grandiose scale, if you will. This criticism applies with most force to the more overtly contractarian approach of Turner, but its logic also extends to affect other interest-theory accounts. Thus, one can similarly argue that Finnis's or Nussbaum's accounts may provide a set of reasons why I should enjoy access to the conditions for basic flourishing or basic goods, but it does not similarly explain why I should act to ensure these conditions are enjoyed by everyone. It lacks an account of justice sufficient for justifying the distribution of resources in a currently deeply unequal world.

As an account of human rights, the interest theory approach generally has to extend its application beyond the parameters of more parochially conceived contractarian political theories, and must aim to identify both a set of fundamental interests we all share and the means by which these may be adequately secured for all. Interest theorists cannot be blamed for the existence of tangible obstacles to the realisation of their principal ends. However, it is reasonable to demand from them some account of how these may be overcome. This is largely absent from the interest theory approach. Within a globally unjust world, the enjoyment of some human rights (such as a right to receive methadone in prison) is likely to appear little more than a social privilege to those whose fundamental human rights are systematically denied every waking day. The interest theory approach rightly stresses the fact of our embodiment as an essential feature of being human. Its focus upon physiological and social attributes generates a relatively robust account of essential interests. The interest theory approach, in general, does a relatively good job at defining what being human consists of. However, the central weakness lies in generating a realisable and politically effective reciprocal commitment to all peoples' human rights out of a vision of what any single individual must have access to if he or she is to be human in the first place. This will require not just a means by which the geo-political barriers between the haves and the have-nots may be overcome, but it will also require a determination of the scope of human rights so that one individual's human right does not become another's mere social privilege. Does the choice theory approach fare any better in determining the basis and scope of human rights?

LIBERTY AND EQUALITY: CHOICE THEORY APPROACH

The pursuit of human rights is driven by a profound ambition: the establishment of a set of material conditions by which each and every human being may enjoy the fundamental protection offered by the gamut of human rights. Fully realising the ambition of human rights can be achieved only once the human rights of all human beings are adequately secured and free from systematic abuse and restriction. This chapter is concerned to analyse those theoretical attempts to identify and justify the basis and scope of human rights claims. We are seeking an account which is capable of avoiding confusing social privileges for human rights. So far, I have argued that the interest-theory approach provides a substantive account of what being human consists of, but fails satisfactorily to confront the challenge presented by a world which falls very far short of securing the fundamental interests of all. The ambition of human rights places very heavy demands upon any normative attempt to justify the doctrine. Essentially it requires identifying the basis upon which any individual's legitimate claims to the enjoyment of human rights secures the legitimacy of all individuals' claims to their human rights. It also requires delineating the scope of any individual's exercise of human rights consistently with all other individuals' potential for exercising their human rights. This challenge may be understood as an attempt to square the circle of two normative ideals which have been essential to the development of human rights and which are also central to the choice theory approach: individual liberty and equality.

Within the theory of human rights the ideals of individual liberty and equality effectively complement one another. However, the two ideals have separate historical developments and separate conceptual structures. Equality has become predominantly understood as non-discrimination, so that all individuals are accorded an equal moral and legal standing within the principal legal and political institutions of modern states. From a human rights perspective, individuals' claim to equal standing is not based upon merit or accomplishment: we do not earn our equality; we possess it inalienably. Nor should any individual's standing be determined by features such as race, gender, ethnicity, physical capabilities, religious or ideological commitments. While a commitment to securing human rights does not, necessarily, require political authorities being 'blind' to such distinctions, it does require the eradication of disadvantage and discrimination on these grounds. The ideal of equality is central to many modern societies. However, it would be fair to say that individual liberty enjoys a somewhat higher profile. Thus, appeals and references to liberty are ubiquitous in modern societies, from the pronouncements of politicians to the marketing of mass consumer commodities. The very ubiquity of the ideal threatens to obscure an understanding of the nature of individual liberty. This is not a purely theoretical concern. The ideal of individual liberty figures prominently in the constitutions of many countries with otherwise very poor human rights records. Identifying the abuse of an ideal entails the possession of a clear understanding of its genuine character and form.

Theoretical understandings of individual liberty owe much to the distinction drawn by the political philosopher, Isaiah Berlin (1969). Berlin distinguishes between two conceptions of liberty, which he refers to as negative liberty and positive liberty. Negative liberty consists primarily in non-interference in an individual's private sphere. Berlin writes, 'I am normally said to be free to the degree to which no man or body of men interferes with my activity. Political liberty in this sense is simply the area within which a man can act unobstructed by others' (1969: 122). We are negatively free to the extent that our actions and thoughts are not directed or unduly coerced by some external agent or institution. Negative liberty expresses what we can call the condition of liberty. That is to say, to enjoy negative liberty is to possess the untrammelled capacity for being free. By contrast, positive liberty expresses and refers to the exercise or actualisation of this condition. Logically speaking, negative liberty's focus upon restricting the interference of others says nothing about what we actually do (or do not do) with this condition. One can, in this sense, enjoy negative liberty and never lift a solitary finger. This is a manifestly incomplete account of human agency, lacking as it does the distinctly 'active' element of human agency. Thus, positive liberty is evidenced by an agent formulating and pursuing goals and projects, the formation and the pursuit of which have not been unduly determined or influenced by externally coercive forces. Individual liberty then consists of these two essential elements: the condition of non-interference and the ability to exercise liberty through the active formulation and pursuit of goals and projects. Having established the very broad features of both equality and individual liberty it is now time to turn directly to that theory of human rights which places greatest emphasis upon these two ideals as determining both the basis and the scope of human rights: the choice theory approach.

The choice theory approach differs from the interest theory approach primarily by the emphasis placed upon the free exercise of choice as the foundation-stone for human rights. Choice theorists refrain from speculating upon the substantive constitution of our nature and focus instead upon the capacity for individual liberty as the distinguishing feature of human-kind. On this account, to be a human agent is to possess both the condition of liberty and sufficient opportunities for exercising one's liberty. If we have a fundamental interest, it is an interest in individual liberty: the value of all other interests is determined by this end. The purpose of human rights is to secure and promote the exercise of free choice. There is no question that the ideal of liberty is central to the human rights doctrine. However, a concern for human rights is not merely for individual liberty *per se*, but for equal individual liberty. Choice theorists aim to identify the basis of this condition and to determine the scope of its application. The most sophisticated and detailed formulation of choice theory is to be found in the work of the American philosopher, Alan Gewirth.

Gewirth's contributions to human rights theory are profound and far-reaching. He presents, arguably, one of the most ambitious accounts of the status and importance of human rights. He states, unequivocally, that 'human rights are derived from the necessary conditions of human action' (1982: x). He continues, 'human rights are of supreme importance and are central to all other moral considerations, because they are the rights of every human being to the necessary conditions of human action; i.e. those conditions that must be fulfilled if human action is to be possible either at all or with general chances of success in achieving the purposes for which humans act' (1982: 3). In effect, he argues that being human entails the possession of human rights.

Gewirth argues that we are all moral agents. We all possess certain purposes and goals, which we wish to see realised. This is an inherent feature of human agency, something we all share. He proceeds to argue that reason demands that we are committed to the view that we must accept the necessity of access to the basic means for satisfying the realisation of our purposes, and that we are logically bound to accept that all such agents must similarly enjoy access to the means for satisfying their basic goals and purposes. Gewirth formulates the details of this argument in what he refers to as the principle of generic consistency (PGC). He identifies what he considers to be four logically necessary steps to a conclusion which holds that we are bound to accept the necessity of human rights by virtue of being rationally purposive agents (1982: 20). These four steps are as follows:

1. Every agent holds that the purposes for which he or she acts are good.
2. Every agent must logically accept the legitimacy of freedom and well-being as necessary conditions for purposive action.
3. Every agent must hold that he or she has rights to freedom and well-being, since denying this is to accept the legitimacy of others interfering in one's actions.
4. Every agent is a purposive agent and rights to freedom and well-being are prerequisite to this condition.

Gewirth concludes this formulation with what he considers to be a dialectically necessary claim (as opposed to a merely assertoric one) by stating that 'my argument for the existence of human rights is that every agent logically must hold or accept that he and all other agents have these rights because their objects are the necessary conditions of human action' (1982: 20).

Gewirth argues then that human rights are the essential means for securing the realisation of our goals, and that having and realising goals is what makes us human agents in the first place. Having claimed that we are rationally bound to accept that all agents enjoy access to these means, Gewirth argues that this demonstrates that all rational agents are logically bound to accept that all rational agents should possess fundamental human rights. In this respect, he insists that we are all both respondents and subjects of rights. Being a moral agent entails enjoying access to the necessary conditions of human agency and a simultaneous obligation to respect (and if necessary to provide for) other agents' possession of these fundamental prerequisites of agency. Ultimately, he claims that for any individual to see oneself as a rational agent is necessarily to acknowledge that one shares a basic character with all other rational agents, and that this recognition entails a necessary acceptance of human rights for all such agents as the very means for being an agent. One may deny human rights to others, but, in so doing, one is acting irrationally in the deepest sense. Thus, he states that a denial by any agent that any or all other agents possess human rights is 'a failure of rationality' (1982: 21). While he accepts

that this happens all of the time in the real world, Gewirth claims to have
provided a definitively logical and rational justification for human rights
which precedes considerations of politics, feelings or religion etc.

This appeal to the apparent force of logic is also clearly apparent in many
of the central elements and concepts of his argument. Thus, he views freedom
and well-being as constituents of action, rather than particular normatively
attributed consequences or results of action. He defines freedom as 'control-
ling one's behaviour by one's unforced choice while having knowledge of
relevant circumstances, with a view to achieving some purpose for which one
acts' (1982: 15). Similarly, in respect of his concept of well-being, he distinguishes between three levels of goods that are constitutive of well-being:
basic, non-substractive and additive (1982: 55–56). The first consists of the
essential preconditions of action, the second of abilities and conditions for
maintaining one's level of purposive action and the third refers to abilities and
conditions for increasing one's level of purposive action. He insists that these
are all inherent and necessary aspects of human agency and owe nothing to the
particular or partial outlook or commitments of any single agent, including, of
course, himself as author of this account.

The style and the general orientation of Gewirth's account of the basis and
scope of human rights has its origins in the rationalist moral philosophy of the
Eighteenth Century German philosopher, Immanuel Kant (Kant, 1964; 1993).
Like Kant, Gewirth claims to have identified a set of principles which apply
to all rational agents as such and are thus binding upon all such agents, at least
in theory. This represents an attempt to identify the grounds upon which I, you
and every other such rational agent may claim to possess human rights: the
grounds for my possession of human rights logically commit me to accept that
all other such agents also possess human rights. The theory aims to combine
individual liberty and equality as fundamentally reciprocal ideals, whilst
purporting to have identified the grounds upon which all moral agency everywhere is constituted. Finally, like Kant's moral philosophy, it is also a version
of philosophical foundationalism. Indeed, one might describe Gewirth as the
definitive rights-foundationalist of the contemporary age.

Gewirth's theory of human rights and his account of rational moral agency
have attracted significant criticism from various quarters. Some have objected
more broadly to any foundationalist moral philosophies. On this view, foundationalism represents a refusal to engage with the social and historical origins
of morality. The anti-foundationalist critique ultimately denies that there are
any trans-historical human truths and no conceptual foundation is ever truly
secure. Gewirth has also been criticised more directly on the ground that his
focus upon purposive agency as the ground for possessing human rights effectively serves to deny human rights to all those human beings who have perma-
nently lost the capacity for purposive deliberation and action: the so-called

marginal cases. However, my critical focus takes a slightly different angle from both of these.

Taken at face value, Gewirth's theory of human rights appears to satisfy the ambition of human rights: to identify the basis for all human beings' possession of fundamental rights, whilst also indicating the grounds upon which the scope of their application may be determined through the combination of liberty and equality. If human rights exist at all, they must adhere to essential features of humankind. Focusing upon the attributes of human agency is a perfectly reasonable place to construct an account capable of expressing the primacy of human rights. If human rights are legitimately to exist at all they must not be based upon and consist of what might be termed value-added extras of human life, but must be fundamental to, if not constitutive of, being human in the first place. Gewirth's account of human rights appears to have grasped and assimilated this aspect of human rights.

His theory would also appear to have dealt more effectively with the so-called motivational question than his interest theory counterparts. For him, the exercise of choice is essential to human agency but is limited to the extent that any agent's exercise of choice is consistent with every other agent's opportunity also to enjoy their liberty. On his highly rationalist reading of the human condition, Gewirth insists that reason itself serves to identify the grounds for supporting the rights of self and other. For him, to be an agent entails necessarily accepting that all agents enjoy access to that which constitutes agency in the first place: fundamental human rights. He states, 'what for any agent are necessarily goods of action, namely freedom and well-being are equally necessary goods for his recipients, and he logically must admit that they have as much right to these goods as he does, since the ground or reason for which he rationally claims them for himself also pertains to his recipients' (1982: 53). He presents a very neat, in places quite beautifully consistent, account of human rights, but ultimately an account which leaves too many important questions unanswered for the purposes of identifying both the basis and the scope of human rights. Two areas are particularly pertinent to this claim: his formulation of reason in the contemporary age and his premise concerning the centrality of human rights to human agency. I shall consider each in turn.

A failure by a human rights theorist to place sufficient importance upon reason as a human faculty would be worthy of criticism, but that does not, of course, apply to the rationalism of Gewirth. However, despite his appeals to the authority of logic, Gewirth's account of the rationality of human rights is inadequate to the modern world in which human rights must secure their existence. If it is a failure of rationality to accept and respect the rights of all other moral agents, then countless millions of human agents must be condemned as irrational. We presently live in a world within which the principal motive for human rights consists in their being systemically abused in sometimes highly planned and complex ways: human rights possess a distinctly reactionary character in environments where they are systematically abused. Understanding how this occurs requires knowledge of many things, foremost of which is the role which power plays in determining the fate of people's lives. Gewirth's rationalism owes much to the systematic character of his thought and, perhaps, the comfort of his study, but largely appears to ignore the social, political and economic realities of the modern world. Representing those realities as significantly irrational is ultimately unhelpful to understanding them better in the aim of overcoming them in order to secure human rights more effectively.

One might conceivably defend Gewirth's strategy here by arguing that he is ultimately concerned to identify the definitive justifications for the very existence of human rights. On this view, the counterpart to transcending the debased character of material reality is to succumb to it, so that the grounds for and parameters of one's proposed rational remedy are themselves unduly infected by the very condition they purport to diagnose and overcome. This line of criticism has been levelled at all those theorists who view reason and rationality as a manifestation of power, principal amongst which are the so-called Nietzscheans and Foucauldians. For many defenders of human rights the essential purpose of the doctrine is to impose constraints and limits upon the exercise of power. Identifying a rational basis and purpose to human rights in this context will serve only to contradict its presumed *raison d'être*. If securing the conditions for equal liberty is central to the very purpose of human rights, then the doctrine must not become a mere manifestation of power in a world beset by deep divisions and inequalities. To this extent, justifications of the basis and scope of human rights must extend to include a formulation of reason as a central element of human agency. If it is to retain its critical purchase, this account of reason must be sufficiently robust and detailed to confront existing realities without either simply reducing to those realities or avoiding engagement with them through an appeal to logic, which lacks a worldly realisation. This is a daunting task and remains a deep challenge for theorists of human rights.[5] An account of reason which effectively dismisses as irrational all thought and action that is not supportive of human rights is not particularly helpful in this regard.

The second area of criticism I focus upon concerns Gewirth's claims regarding the centrality of human rights to human agency. This line of criticism extends upon the basis established by that which raises concerns for how human rights may justifiably be extended to cover human beings who have

---

[5]   I engage with this challenge in respect of contemporary liberal political morality. See my *Demoralising Liberalism: T.W. Adorno and Contemporary Liberal Philosophy* (Palgrave, forthcoming).

lost the capacity for purposive agency insofar as it concerns both the purported logical character of his claims and recognising that all human life is not based upon the satisfactory establishment of human rights.

Gewirth insists that his claims are not assertoric. He insists that his account is not simply yet another purely normative depiction of how things ought to be according to the prejudices and outlook of the author. He describes his defence of human rights as a form of metaethics which transcends separate substantive and more partial ethical perspectives (1982: 45–46). Indeed, he argues that the logical basis of his central claims derive their origins from the very basis and structure of morality itself. He appeals to what he considers to be, in effect, the very DNA of morality: the necessary conditions for freedom and wellbeing. Unlike other accounts of human rights, Gewirth views his own account as having overcome the partiality and perspectival limitations of mere ethics. When he cracks open the core of human morality he finds human rights. To appreciate the basis and force of this second line of criticism it is imperative to recognise the extent of Gewirth's claims and ambition in this regard.

Put simply, it is manifestly wrong to claim that human rights are prerequisites for human agency *per se*: they are not. It might seem normatively desirable to attempt to extend their importance in this way but it is not empirically sustainable. Human life has proceeded and continues to proceed in many places without the protection and enjoyment of human rights. Too much of human life comprises the abuse of human rights, but if one takes away the fundamental rights human life does not thereby simply dissolve into some purportedly logical contradiction. One might be intellectually charitable to Gewirth and assume he means that a right to life is fundamental to human life; this seems far less controversial, if a little unduly self-evident. However, his account of human rights extends to include conditions for freedom and for wellbeing. His account thus extends far beyond a mere right to life. The relevance of this particular line of criticism is not so much that Gewirth falsely represents human empirical reality: he cannot genuinely think that wherever one finds human agency one will also find secure human rights. I do not base this criticism of his work on this claim, but rather upon what he indicates about the nature of his attempt to justify human rights. The defence of human rights is based not upon identifying the conditions for human life, but upon identifying the conditions for a certain quality of life. As I shall argue in greater detail in the following chapter, the human rights doctrine is inherently and necessarily evaluative in its approach towards both the basis and the scope of human rights. This is crucial to understanding human rights and essential to any attempt to justify human rights claims. One cannot escape this, despite its attractions at times, by appealing to logic or to 'life' without thereby dissolving the capacity of human rights to hold certain forms of life to critical account. Gewirth provides a highly ambitious and intellectually complex

account of human rights. However, his argument is subject to significant criticism, which serves to undermine the theory's ability adequately to gauge the
role human rights have to play in securing human agency. Like its interest
theory counterpart, choice theory leaves us begging too many questions and
fails to provide sufficient answers for the purposes of fully determining the
basis and scope of human rights. This may be illustrated by returning to the
distinction drawn earlier between human rights and social privileges.

INTEREST AND CHOICE IN THE REALM OF RIGHTS AND PRIVILEGES

Interest and choice-theory approaches to human rights aim to identify the basis
and scope of human rights. They both aspire, in slightly different ways, to
identify essential attributes of humankind and human agency. I have argued
that identifying the basis of human rights claims entails a delineation of the
scope of their application also: we ought to have rights to what make us fundamentally human agents. While such an approach is essential to the theory of
human rights, it is also deeply complex. Human beings disagree over what our
natures may be. They also disagree fundamentally over how far anyone's
moral obligations to others must extend. Likewise, identifying what is a
genuinely 'free' action is fraught with normative complexity. I have argued
that neither interest theory nor Gewirth's choice theory has succeeded yet in
providing a fully water-tight justification for determining the basis and scope
of human rights.

   To return to the distinction drawn between human rights and social privileges, one can discern how both theoretical approaches may themselves be
vulnerable to the so-called phenomenon of human rights inflationism, which
confuses privileges with rights. This is particularly pronounced in the context
of global geo-political inequalities. As I will discuss in greater detail in
Chapters 2 and 3, the moral essence of human rights is a commitment to the
distribution of the resources necessary for their enjoyment within a global
community. When seen from this perspective, however, we are confronted by
a world of human rights haves and have-nots. The trend towards human rights
inflationism is, not surprisingly, most pronounced amongst the so-called
haves: populations of the economically wealthy nations, mostly but not exclusively situated in the Northern hemisphere.[6] Legal and moral claims to human
rights made amongst these populations on the basis of, for example, equal

---

   [6]   The phenomenon of global inequality will be discussed in far greater detail in
Chapter 6.

liberty are liable to appear as claims to mere social privileges amongst those who must confront malnutrition and politically oppressive regimes. The present organisation of states and the attribution of principal human rights obligations to individual nation-states serve to compound this discrepancy through establishing a very much higher threshold of minimal conditions amongst the haves than for our have-not counterparts. Absolute discrepancies cannot be overcome: one does require more resources for establishing a life of minimal freedom and wellbeing in wealthy societies than in poor ones. However, rising expectations and associated claims to human rights amongst wealthy nations will not serve to promote the fundamental human rights of those other members of the human family unfortunate enough to live beyond the boundaries of affluence. Human rights inflationism is positively detrimental to human rights when viewed from a global perspective.

What is required then is a means for distinguishing between human rights and social privileges. As embodied beings we have a collection of fundamental interests in our physiological wellbeing and security. As social beings, we have a collection of interests in the establishment and maintenance of material conditions conducive to and supportive of our existence as distinct moral agents. Finally, the capacity for reflexive self-consciousness grounds our potential for deliberating upon the conditions of our lives and for desiring that these conditions comply with our self-interpretations: individual and collective freedom entails the capacity for determining what these interpretations are and for, when necessary, changing the material conditions of our lives so as to realise them, rather than frustrate them. Taken together, the interest and choice-theory approaches provide the ground for developing an understanding of human rights which does not succumb to excessive partiality in the claims of some over others. We have a shared basis in our claims to human rights in the first instance. This commonality should serve to determine the legitimate scope of the application of these claims. However, neither account has, as yet, satisfactorily provided such an account. The distinction between human rights and social privileges, when viewed from the global perspective of human rights, remains an obstacle to their realisation.

TOWARDS AN ALTERNATIVE: SUFFERING AND A MINIMALLY GOOD LIFE

Human rights enjoy unequivocal moral authority when responding to gross human suffering. In many respects, human rights have become a veritable paradigmatic discourse for defining systematic human suffering. I have written elsewhere (Fagan, 2008) of the need for human rights theorists not to lose sight of this fact. In a world still far too beset by systematic human suffering the central value of human rights is, unfortunately, reactionary and condemnatory, rather than regulatory and celebratory. Any attempt adequately to distinguish between human rights and social privileges must begin with determining what constitutes human suffering. Some forms of human suffering are, so to speak, relatively self-evidently so; genocide is the obvious example. However, the doctrine of human rights would be severely limited if it were to stop there. One can take this further and argue that, whilst seeking to prevent systematic human suffering ought to provide the initial stimulus for human rights, it should not be the end-point of the doctrine's application: our common attributes extend beyond suffering. Taking the scope of the doctrine further raises, however, the relativistic spectre encountered previously in seeking to distinguish between one person's right and another person's privilege. In a world less beset by such widespread suffering and misery it would be morally churlish to suggest that such a distinction might be drawn by appealing to more minimally-inclined criteria: where we set the threshold must be informed by and respond to current material conditions. To this end, I conclude this chapter by referring to James Nickel's notion of human rights as means for securing the conditions for a minimally good life (1987: 51).

Nickel defends the human rights doctrine as a form of minimal moral perfectionism. Human rights are thereby presented as encompassing a conception of what a minimally desirable human life must comprise. This extends to include the physiological, social and rationally deliberative elements I referred to above. However, as a form of minimal moral perfectionism, human rights do not extend to determining everything that may be considered good and desirable for fully active agents. Rather, the doctrine aims to establish a minimal threshold below which a minimally good life is not possible. Given the global perspective of human rights, this threshold must necessarily be universalised and will require the setting of standards which, whilst sensitive to 'local' conditions, do not serve ultimately to exacerbate discrepancies between human rights haves and have-nots. Nickel's concept of a minimal threshold may not, ultimately, overcome the inherently evaluative character of attempts to define the basis and scope of humankind and our correlative rights. It does offer us, for the time being at least, a more satisfactory criterion by which we may begin to separate rights from privileges.

CONCLUSION

This chapter has addressed a relatively common misunderstanding concerning the scope of human rights and the distinction between human rights and social privileges. I have argued that engaging with this misunderstanding entails an analysis of the theoretical attempts to identify the basis and scope of the legitimate application of human rights. I have argued that, as they stand, neither interest theory nor choice theory proves entirely satisfactory in establishing an equitable demarcation between rights and privileges. I have also argued that the distinction must be drawn in a manner consistent with the global perspective of human rights and a concern for all human beings' fundamental rights. Finally, whilst acknowledging the difficulty in overcoming some of the obstacles to pinning down a secure distinction between rights and privileges, I have proposed that a more constructive place to develop such an account lies in a re-engagement with systematic human suffering as a central motive for human rights and, beyond this, an account of human rights as a form of minimal moral perfectionism. At this point in time, these latter claims remain unduly assertive and insufficiently detailed. A number of essential questions require answering, including questions concerning the analytical structure of rights, what moral standing do human rights possess, what is the basis of their moral validity, which forms of political institutions are most consistent with realising human rights as means for securing a minimally good life, and others besides. The remaining chapters aim to provide answers to these questions whilst fleshing out the substantive account of human rights I propose. Chapter 2 focuses upon the analytical structure of rights and their moral standing.

2. Human rights and law's domain

INTRODUCTION

This chapter is principally concerned to address the question of what, if anything, authorises human rights principles. The question is addressed by means of a critical analysis of a long-established and widely held myth concerning the predominance of law within the theory and practice of human rights. Specifically, the myth holds that human rights can ultimately be understood only as distinctly legal phenomena because human rights can really be said to exist only as legal entities. On this view, human rights principles are authorised by law through achieving legal recognition and codification. This view is most closely associated with legal positivism. It would be foolish to deny that law figures prominently in our understanding and practising human rights. It would also be foolish to deny that legal positivism has exerted a lasting and significant influence upon the development of liberal jurisprudence which, in turn, has significantly influenced human rights. This influence has been most pronounced within the practice of human rights. However, the myth of law's sufficiency in authorising human rights principles needs to be challenged on several fronts and for several different reasons. This chapter aims to achieve this by demonstrating some of the limitations of a legal-positivist approach to the theory and practice of human rights, before proceeding to analyse the distinctly moral basis and character of human rights as a distinct doctrine. This will involve a consideration of the historical development of the concept of moral rights which pre-exist, or exist independently of, distinct and 'positive' legal systems. I then proceed to consider various moral perspectives upon the concept of human rights as moral rights, foremost of which will be moral realism. I argue that morality is a fundamental element of the theory and practice of human rights. However, admitting morality's role also raises serious issues for understanding human rights. I argue that morality possesses an inherently reflexive character and that the character of morality confronts us with a challenge: how to achieve consensus and agreement in the face of empirical moral disagreement. This challenge then provides a focal point for Chapter 3. In order to provide a clear understanding of what is ultimately the object of dispute, I begin Chapter 2, however, with a discussion of the analytical and substantive properties of rights.

CONCEPTUAL AND SUBSTANTIVE PROPERTIES AND DISTINCTIONS

There is sometimes a tendency to speak of a 'right' in relatively simplified terms, which assumes that any right is ultimately a singular, undifferentiated entity. In actual fact, a 'right' is a term that covers a complex range of internally differentiated properties and elements. Also, the substantive objects of rights are differentiated in ways which have a clear bearing on understanding how and by whom they may be authorised. Let us begin with the conceptual properties of a right.

First and foremost, a right correlates with a related duty. The possession and exercise of a right presupposes a relation with some other agent or institution who or which is charged with the duty of ensuring the right-holder's enjoyment of his or her right. This relationship between rights and duties is often referred to as the 'correlativity thesis'.[1] Second, rights (and duties) may be analytically divided between negative and positive rights (Jones, 1994). Negative rights are formally very similar to Berlin's conception of negative liberty, which was analysed in the previous chapter. A negative right imposes a duty upon others to refrain from interfering with one's body, thought or action. Thus, a right to be free from torture imposes a duty upon others not to inflict torture upon those who bear the right. In contrast, a positive right imposes a duty upon others to provide some resource or opportunity which is a prerequisite for the exercise of a particular right. An example would be a right to health or education. A right to either health or education can be adequately realised and enjoyed only through the active provision of health-care services and sufficiently resourced schools. A negative right to either health or education would restrict others from preventing the right-holder from seeking such services but would entail no duty actually to provide the necessary services in the first instance. We can say that the very nature or object of some rights requires the imposition of positive duties upon others if the right is to be adequately realised in the first place. One should be careful, however, not unduly to reify the distinction between negative and positive rights. There are rights and instances where both negative and positive elements are constitutive of the exercise of the right. The best example of this is the right to life. A right to life obviously imposes negative duties upon others not to take it away, but also imposes positive duties upon others to provide for the essential resources of life, such as access to water, shelter, health-care and the like

---

[1]   The correlation of rights and duties has significant effects upon our understanding and exercise of human rights. I will devote the whole of Chapter 6 to an analysis of this relationship.

(Hunt, 1996). A further distinction to be made concerns so-called rights *in rem* and rights *in personam* (Hohfeld, 1978). Rights *in rem* impose duties (either negative or positive) upon an undifferentiated community of others: a right to freedom of conscience imposes a duty upon all others to refrain from seeking to restrict any individual's fundamental beliefs and commitments. By contrast, a right *in personam* imposes a duty upon some particular class or category of agents to provide for that right. A right to education is thus correlated with those public authorities who are charged with providing an adequate educational system. It would be somewhat odd and most likely rather counter-productive indiscriminately to charge everyone with this particular duty.

It is clear that the very concept of a right is complex and multi-faceted. This is even more apparent when one shifts focus to include all of those human rights included within such fundamental documents as the Universal Declaration of Human Rights (UDHR). That category of entities we refer to as human rights can itself be further sub-divided into at least two distinct categories of human rights: civil and political, and economic, social and cultural rights. This distinction has been codified within international human rights law with the establishment of the two principal human rights covenants: the International Covenant on Civil and Political Rights (ICCPR) and the International Covenant on Economic, Social and Cultural Rights (ICESCR). It is also possible to identify a further distinction between economic and social rights *and* cultural rights. The basis for this distinction is both historical and substantive. Thus some theorists have identified three progressive generations of rights, which consist of civil and political, economic and social, and finally cultural rights (Freeman, 2002). Substantively, it has also been argued that cultural rights have a more overtly collectivist character than their earlier two predecessors and are substantively different in this respect (Freeman, 1995). These claims are important and will be discussed further in the next chapter. For the moment, however, I will retain a focus upon the distinction made legally concrete by the two principal covenants.

Thus, while the substantive distinction offered above is well-founded upon existing human rights literature and practice, the distinctions themselves and the relative weight attached to them have attracted controversy. Thus, some have argued that genuine human rights do not extend beyond the civil and political category of rights (Cranston, 1973; Nozick, 1974). This line of reasoning also draws heavily upon a distinction between negative and positive rights, whereby the former are associated with civil and political rights and the latter with their economic and social counterparts. Put simply, civil and political rights are said to comprise primarily negative rights, while economic, social and cultural rights are considered to be mostly positive in character. Both Maurice Cranston and Robert Nozick have argued in their respective ways that legitimate human rights claims can extend to include negative civil and political rights only. Both theorists endorsed a wider political end of limiting the power of the state to interfere and intercede in individuals' lives. Both were very wary of what they considered to be paternalistically motivated attempts to attribute a greater range of essential duties to the state in providing for the economic, social and cultural well-being and interests of those subject to the state's authority. The greater the range of positive duties attributed to the state, the greater would be the need for the state to extend its services, and with them its power to provide for the correlative positive rights. Both Cranston and Nozick argued that the highly undesirable end of increasing state power could be effectively avoided by restricting individuals' rights to cover only negative civil and political rights, such as a (negatively envisaged) right to life, a right against torture, a right to privacy, and a right to private property (amongst others). Cranston also argued that it was simply far easier uncontroversially to determine that a negative civil and political right had been realised, in contrast to an economic, social and cultural counterpart. The latter, he argued, possessed an inherently indeterminate character which prevented a clear determination of, for example, precisely what level of health care or education is sufficient to satisfy a right to health or education.

On an initial reading, the concerns of Cranston and Nozick may appear to resonate with those addressed in the previous chapter. There are several good reasons to be wary of an over-inflation of the discourse of human rights, and the extent to which the state is the principal body charged with human rights duties should also encourage some consideration before seeking to extend the provision of human rights duties. However, Cranston's and Nozick's ideologically motivated analytical distinction between negative civil and political and positive economic, social and cultural rights is ultimately unsustainable in the light of the actualisation of many rights, both civil and political and economic, social and cultural. As I stated above, a right to life (arguably the essential human right) cannot ultimately be configured in exclusively negative or positive terms. Being able to exercise the right to life requires not just being free from murder but also having access to those resources that are essential to maintaining life. In this respect, a right to life necessarily comprises both negative and positive elements. It will also, thereby, entail the provision of civil and political and economic, social and cultural rights. A similar observation applies to an attempt to sustain a fundamental distinction between the two categories of rights. In some cases, what appears to belong unambiguously to one category of right may actually involve the assimilation of elements from the other category and thereby confuses any hard and fast distinction. The ostensibly civil and political right to vote, for example, also entails the capacity to exercise judgement and to be sufficiently educated about the political system to which one belongs. It will also require a level of health that does not prevent one from exercising one's judgement and casting one's vote. To borrow a term introduced by Henry Shue (1996), one may say that many rights are rather more *holistic* in character than the distinction between the two categories would suggest. There are good reasons to seek to restrict the scope of human rights, but this cannot be achieved by seeking to enforce a false analytical and substantive distinction between rights. Returning to the criterion introduced towards the end of Chapter 1, securing the conditions for leading a minimally good life will necessarily entail the provision of both civil and political rights and economic, cultural and social rights. It will also involve recognising that many rights will be both negative and positive in character. We may proceed then with a conception of a right which includes a distinction between negative and positive rights, correlates rights with duties, and distinguishes between different categories of rights in respect of who is identified as possessing the duty to provide for the right. Our understanding of what rights consist of will also extend to include both civil and political and economic, social and cultural rights. Having established some common object of discussion, we must now turn to the questions of how human rights achieve a legitimate and authorised existence.

LEGAL-POSITIVISM AND THE AUTHORIAL POWER OF THE LAW

I have argued that the fundamental purpose of human rights is to secure the necessary conditions for each individual human being leading a minimally good life. I have also demonstrated that each human right correlates with a corresponding duty, so that none of us can be said to enjoy or possess any of our human rights in a purely solitary condition: the existence of human rights presupposes human relationships. This has undoubtedly influenced a stream of thought which holds that human rights are legitimised and even created only through the mechanisms of legitimate and sovereign law-makers. Put simply, human rights depend upon law for their existence and their application. This stream of thought is both well-established and long-standing and is generally referred to as legal-positivism.

   Legal-positivism owes its historical origins to the Nineteenth Century English philosopher Jeremy Bentham. Bentham (1987) formulated the terms of legal positivism by means of a critique of the idea that rights can be legitimately said to exist and command moral authority prior to or outside legal recognition and a legal framework. His critique rests upon an epistemological argument and a political claim. Bentham argued that the only legitimate form of law was positive law: law which emanated from an identifiable sovereign authority. The counterpart to positive law was so-called natural law. Natural law will be discussed further in the next section, but for the moment it suffices to know that natural law posits the existence of forms of justice and rights which exist independently of any tangible political or legal institution or configuration. The tenets of natural law thereby provide a resource for criticising and opposing existing codified law. In countering natural law, Bentham insisted that the very concepts of natural law and natural rights were epistemologically nonsensical and false. Drawing upon a correspondence theory of truth, Bentham insisted that no such entities actually existed beyond the realm of the imagination of natural lawyers. On this view, law is, by definition, that which has been recognised by a sovereign law-making authority. Those rights which have been so recognised can be said thereby legitimately to exist as law, whereas those which have not cannot claim any authority over us. Rights are authorised by law. In addition, Bentham also argued that the idea of natural law was politically harmful and subversive of sovereign legal authorities. Echoing the criticisms levelled by Edmund Burke at the French Revolution, Bentham argued that societies have an inherent interest in peace and stability. A principal means for achieving this was provided by law which originated from a single, sovereign authority. Natural law represents an obvious threat to the continuing legitimacy of sovereign authority by claiming an independently legitimate existence.

In respect of his epistemological claim, Bentham argues, in effect, that there are no such things as moral facts, as natural lawyers insisted. The fabric of the world does not contain normative facts. We cannot derive our beliefs about what constitutes a good life from purportedly natural attributes of the human condition. We may be able to identify facts about human life and its prerequisites, but we can never justify our normative evaluation of these conditions purely by appeal to their existence. In making this argument, Bentham was drawing upon the earlier writings of the Scottish Eighteenth Century philosopher David Hume and, in particular, the distinction Hume draws between facts and values. Hume (1975) argued that there existed, in effect, two distinct types of entity: facts and values. He insisted that they were fundamentally distinct phenomena. Facts refer to demonstrable physical properties of the world, whereas values refer to our evaluative beliefs about how the world ought to be. Hume argued that morality was an inherently evaluative phenomenon and that it comprised evaluative beliefs and statements. Moral beliefs and statements can never describe the world, but rather are an expression of the author's own evaluative preferences. Moral confusion arose from mistaking values for facts; from claiming that states of affairs which we may wish to be the case actually are so. In effect, this is precisely what natural law appears to have fallen foul of. In Bentham's terms, legitimate law has a tangible and demonstrable existence. If we want to know which laws and which rights exist we need look no further than legal documentation. Those aspects of the natural law wish-list which are not to be found in legal documents must be understood as inherently evaluative moral preferences.

Subsequent generations of legal theorists have developed Bentham's initial formulation of legal positivism (see Kelsen, 1978; Hart, 1994). The constant element in the development of this general position is an insistence that law and morality are separate phenomena. The authority and legitimacy of law are thereby dependent not upon how accurately any particular piece of legislation complies with related moral beliefs, but rather by appeal to its compliance with the established institutional mechanisms, rules and procedures which govern the particular sovereign authority in question. Law and morality must not be confused with one another.

A contemporary variation of the legal positivist tradition has been labelled 'democratic positivism' (Campbell, 2006). Democratic positivism shares the positivist view of rights as existing only in tangible legal form but attempts to develop a far more sophisticated account of how sovereign legislative authorities can claim to be legitimate in the first place. In effect, democratic positivism seeks to resolve the distinction and separation between facts and values through an account of legitimate legislative authority. The legitimacy of evaluative rights claims is conferred through democratic deliberation and legislation. Thus, it retains a concern to exclude purely evaluative claims from the realm of legitimate law, whilst proposing a particular institutional mechanism through which purely evaluative claims can achieve a tangibly legitimate existence. A commitment is retained, however, to the view that legitimate law is only that which has achieved this status of recognition. The claims of natural law are thereby still rejected. On this view, legitimate rights are legal rights.

The general legal positivist view of human rights should now be clear. From a legal positivist view legitimate human rights are those which have been legally recognised and codified. Human rights exist as legal rights or not at all. Human rights comprise a tangible body of national and international legal instruments, covenants, protocols, treaties and customary law which demonstrably exist. On this legal positivist view of human rights the existence of this tangible body of legal instruments is all one need be concerned with. On a legal positivist view, legitimate law is positive law, law which exists as law and not as merely evaluative projections. The legal positivist view does not deny the 'existence' of moral beliefs concerning the alleged independence of criteria and principles by which positive law can be judged. Legal positivism does not seek to deny the existence of moral beliefs, but merely seeks to set these to one side; outside the realm of law.

Legal positivism has exerted a significant influence upon the manner in which law has been understood and evaluated. In some respects, while I am ultimately claiming it to be a myth, legal positivism contains some ostensive appeal. Thus, it would be churlish to deny the potential power of law to achieve particular ends. Law may often enjoy a degree of legitimacy that transcends more partial moral commitments and beliefs. Law also comprises a series of instruments and mechanisms for seeking to realise particular ends. The international law of human rights is an extensive body, which covers a very wide range of human rights and seeks to offer protection to a vast constituency of human beings. Supporters of human rights have every reason to seek to transform their aspirations and desires into tangible legal form, and the gap between moral aspiration and legal codification appears to be, as Louis Henkin (1990) has argued, ever-diminishing. Given the undoubted benefits of legal support and Henkin's claim that the gap between morality and law is growing ever smaller in respect of human rights claims, one might feel justified in concluding that concerns over legal positivism are largely academic and irrelevant to our understanding and practice of human rights. If legal positivism is guilty of perpetuating a myth of law's sufficiency for understanding and practising human rights, the myth has nevertheless become real.

Without seeking to question the importance of law for human rights, the claims made on behalf of legal positivism are worthy of criticism, and on two distinct fronts: first, in respect of the claim concerning the ever-diminishing division between human rights principles and their legal codification and, second, in respect of the manner in which legal positivism characterises positive law.

As has been already acknowledged, the international law of human rights is a growing body of documentation and institutions. Those sovereign nation-states which have yet to ratify the principal human rights instruments constitute a small minority. This has led a number of theorists, including Louis Henkin (1990) and Jack Donnelly (1998), to declare our age an age of human rights. While such pronouncements may positively stir the emotions, we should avoid simply assuming that the human rights 'project' is largely complete. Given the vast range of systematic human rights abuses across the globe, this is manifestly not the case. The myth of legal positivism may prove significantly harmful if we assume that human rights are essentially legal phenomena and that the degree to which they have secured a legal existence testifies to their efficacy. Two issues are particularly relevant in this regard. The first concerns the discrepancy between ratifying and realising human rights instruments. Legally ratified human rights are violated every day across the globe. Within some jurisdictions effective mechanisms of complaint and redress exist, which at least constitute a potential obstacle to continuing abuse. Within other jurisdictions, however, such mechanisms either do not exist or are entirely inadequate. Individuals' legal rights may be violated but nothing follows from this. Thus, the mere existence of legally recognised human rights provides no measure of their actual realisation. The second goes even deeper into this realm of concern and addresses those individual sovereign nation-states which have not recognised specific elements of the international body of human rights law.

The principal global regulatory human rights regime is, of course, the United Nations. While the public ethos of the UN may often appear to be imbued with the spirit of human rights, the organisation's capacity to enforce human rights norms upon member states is constrained in a number of ways. The most important of these is the principle of national sovereignty, which is the fulcrum upon which the UN is based. Thus, national sovereignty is enshrined within the UN Charter. Article 2(7) of the UN Charter prohibits the UN from 'intervening in matters which are essentially the domestic jurisdiction of any state'. This means that, with the exceptions of genocide, a right to life and a right to be free from torture, individual nation-states are under no legal obligation to recognise or implement any other human rights principles. Member states are subject to varying forms of regulatory action once a particular instrument has been ratified, but, with the exception of those above, they are under no compelling obligation to recognise any such instrument. In such cases, adherence to the tenets of legal positivism appears to exclude the possibility of concluding that the human rights of the citizens of any such nation-state are being violated, since no such rights have achieved legal recognition within that particular jurisdiction. We would have to conclude that apartheid South Africa was not based upon the wholesale violation of the majority's human rights. Similarly, we would have to conclude that the lack of access to health-care which afflicts millions of US citizens does not constitute a human rights violation, given the United States' refusal to ratify the ICESCR.

Democratic positivists might object to the above charge, particularly in respect of the South African example. The democratic positivist will insist that the legitimacy of a given jurisdiction will depend upon the establishment of democratic procedures and institutions which serve to validate and authorise the panoply of legal rights. Apartheid South Africa would not be accepted as an example of a legitimate positivist state on this basis. There is an obvious problem with this form of reasoning, however. A commitment to democracy as a prerequisite to determining the legitimacy of ensuing legal rights presupposes that at least those rights which are necessary for democratic participation are excluded from this process; the legitimacy of these rights is simply presupposed, rather than effectively established. This presupposition, desirable though it may well be, is ultimately based upon moral principles and assumptions: morality is thereby re-inscribed at the very core of the positivist vision of legitimate law and provides a basis for criticising and holding to account separate legal jurisdictions which do not recognise democratic rights. A similar issue concerning the moral character of legitimate law underlies the second area of criticism.

The second front upon which legal positivism's view of human rights can be challenged concerns the attempt to distinguish law from morality. To what extent can the legitimacy of law be understood without appeal to moral criteria? Thus, one might respond to the above line of critical reasoning that its conclusions are undermined by the degree to which it rests upon merely normative claims and assumptions. That is to say, one might counter the above claims by saying that their legitimacy rests upon a mere *a priori* assumption that human rights are valid, independently of legal recognition. One might say that this amounts to a mere reassertion of the normative claim in question, and not a demonstration of its validity. As a separate but related form of criticism it might also be said that the above criticisms entail that one must impose morality upon the law and simply assume that this is a legitimate undertaking. How might this retort be responded to?

The most consistently critical and detailed analysis of legal positivism's separation of law and morality has been undertaken by the legal philosopher Ronald Dworkin. The core of his criticism can be found in his 1986 book *Law's Empire*. Dworkin presents a complex vision of the law as a social and moral phenomenon. The essence of his critique of legal positivism consists of his argument that morality is already an inextricable element of law-making. Law and morality are not two distinct phenomena but are bound up with one another in complex, socially informed ways. According to Dworkin, law is not made in some institutional bubble, or sphere that is entirely separate from the social and political contexts of its development and application. In making law legislators, and especially jurists, draw upon existing interpretations of moral values and norms. Dworkin argues that judicial reasoning, in particular, empirically involves a consistent engagement with and reference to not just other laws and judicial decisions but moral principles also. Law draws upon, and helps to construct, the moral fabric of society. The legal positivist is empirically mistaken in claiming that law is separate from morality. Law represents an institutionalised expression of dominant societal and moral values and ideals. While law represents the tangible institutionalisation of moral ideals and values, the resulting product necessarily retains an inherently evaluative character, which enables and sustains a capacity for legitimately criticising positive law for its perceived moral weaknesses or limitations. Dworkin's argument draws upon a long-established property of a perspective from human rights, which posits the potential and need for criticising law for its failure adequately to realise the ambition of human rights. So, the morality of human rights represents one of these sources which law draws upon. Human rights cannot thereby be reduced to law but must continue to pre-exist law. Dworkin's critique of legal positivism points the way back to the need for human rights to retain their status as moral rights in order to avoid the doctrine becoming a mere hostage to the fortune of law's recognition.

The clear implication of the above discussion is that, while law is a powerful mechanism for realising human rights principles, the existence and legitimacy of these principles cannot be reducible to or dependent upon legal recognition. Human rights possess and must maintain an existence and legitimacy which are independent from the law. The myth of legal positivism is potentially so harmful to the extent that it seeks to obscure this fact. Human rights are essentially moral phenomena and the myth is thereby dispelled. While the conclusion regarding legal positivism must stand, the statement regarding the inherently moral character of human rights principles should not be simply accepted as such. In dispelling one myth, we must be careful to avoid simply affirming another. There is very much more to the morality of human rights than is immediately apparent within assertions of their moral character.

MORAL RIGHTS AND THE SEARCH FOR JUSTIFIED MORALITY

The conceptual counterpart to the insistence that the only legitimately existing rights are legal rights is the claim that human rights fundamentally emerge as (and always remain) moral rights. The existence and justification of moral rights are not held to be conditional upon their being legally recognised or politically realised, although both of these are obviously desirable. The theorist Brian Orend defines moral rights as follows: '[m]oral rights need not be written into actual legal codes: maybe they are, maybe not. Moral rights exist either as rights within social moralities or as rights within what we might call a critical, or justified morality. A social morality is a widely believed and practised code of conduct in a given society' (2002: 24). Thus, a right may be simultaneously a moral and a legal right if it has secured legal recognition under some or other jurisdiction. Legal recognition is neither necessary nor sufficient to support the claim that moral rights do tangibly exist. Their existence can be corroborated by reference to existing social moralities. An example of such can be found amid the ideals, values and norms which underlay the formulation of the Universal Declaration of Human Rights. After all the UDHR was clearly not a mere repetition of existing legal rights, but sought to provide the moral fount for the establishment of human rights as a globally binding legal doctrine. As James Nickel has commented, 'in promulgating the Universal Declaration as a "common standard of achievement", the United Nations did not purport to describe rights already recognized everywhere or to enact these rights within international law. Instead, it attempted to set forth the norms that exist within enlightened moralities' (1987: 4). Human rights 'originate' as moral rights in their quest to become legal rights and their continuing status as independent moral rights enables them to provide a source for critically evaluating the progress of the establishment of legally recognised rights.

Pointing to the existence of an established social morality does not suffice to justify the substance and content of the morality in question. After all, a central element of the purpose of moral rights is to counter a naïve empiricism which holds that existence is inherently self-justifying. Thus the operative phrases are contained in the references to 'critical' and 'enlightened' moralities. What do defenders of moral rights have in mind when they appeal to such terms? One must also ask whether moral rights have a distinct historical development. Some readers might discern an apparent tension or even contradiction in formulating these two questions alongside one another. It is often felt that demonstrating the historical basis and development of any moral doctrine serves ultimately to undermine any claims such a doctrine may have towards universal validity. The issue of the purported universal applicability of human rights will be addressed in great detail in the following chapter. It is, nevertheless, important to acknowledge the importance of universality to the defence of moral rights. Without seeking to offer a detailed defence of this claim before the following chapter, I will base my analysis of moral rights and the morality which underlies them on an assumption that no moral doctrine is ever devoid of history. No moral doctrine leaps fully formed from the head of some great moral philosopher and on to the laps of those who seek to establish a global morality based upon respect for fundamental human rights. In discussing the basis and form of moral rights, I will, therefore, consider both their historical development and their justification.

Moral rights essentially rest upon a claim that a justified morality is not merely a reflection of the values and ideals of some particular and partial society or civilisation. Moral rights are held to be valid for all human beings everywhere. This commitment has typically been associated with an insistence that the basis and content of moral rights transcend any given social or cultural community. As moral rights, human rights apply to all human beings, regardless of creed, gender, nationality, ethnicity, social class and all of the other facets of social identity. Thus, defenders of moral rights have consistently argued that there exist trans-historical, asocial and universally valid moral facts, which provide the basis for and serve to orient the content of ensuing moral rights. The existence of these moral facts enables one to identify forms of 'true' and 'genuine' justice which transcend and provide evaluative criteria for all actually existing political, legal and social systems. They provide a set of genuinely independent criteria for identifying what are morally just rights and systems in the first place. Justice is not whatever the powerful declare it to be, nor is it reducible to the particular values or world-view of a specific constituency of human beings.

From its historical beginnings, this way of thinking about justice was associated with challenges to worldly forms of power. Thinkers sought to challenge the claims of the powerful by reference to a set of allegedly 'natural' criteria for justice which necessarily preceded any more artificially constructed rationale for attempting to legitimise the exercise of might. Appeals to so-called natural justice provided a means for challenging the adage that might necessarily makes right. The first group of thinkers to claim the existence of anything resembling naturally enshrined moral rights were the ancient Stoic philosophers. Early Stoics such as Zeno and Cleanthes argued that the good of mankind was to live in accordance with the dictates of nature. An appeal to living in accordance with nature thereby provided a fundamental criterion for evaluating existing legal and political systems. Later Stoics such as the Romans Marcus Aurelius, Seneca and Epictetus developed the doctrine further in a way that expanded the reach of the doctrine to a wider constituency of people (Sharples, 1996). Similarly, the Roman jurist Cicero insisted that there existed true forms of moral justice independently of any given legal or political system and provided criteria for judging the validity of any such system. Morally just legal and political systems were those which complied with the tenets of natural justice and not necessarily with the dictates of political rulers.

This idea is then further developed by Christian theologians in Europe during the Middle Ages, such as Thomas Aquinas and William of Ockham. Aquinas argued that all just law owed its existence to a proper discernment of eternal law, which itself derived from the will of God. We understand God's will through the development and deployment of reason, the very purpose of which is to achieve an understanding of God's will (Aquinas, 1981). For his part, William of Ockham developed an account of rights grounded upon both understanding the will of God through the use of reason and an account of ownership derived from the exercise of an individual's free will. Ockham provides a prototypical account of rights as a means for securing ownership over one's self and one's possessions. The overtly theological development of the concept of natural law provided the basis for the increasing secularisation of an understanding of justice and rights during the Seventeenth and Eighteenth Centuries. Arguably, the most influential of these was to be found in the political philosophy of John Locke, which was to have a profound influence upon the rhetoric of the American and French revolutions of the Eighteenth Century.

Locke epitomises a brand of political philosophy which was essential in the development of what was to become human rights. In his *Two Treatises of Government* (1988) Locke developed a sophisticated account of natural rights which is principally characterised by the claim that there exist certain fundamental natural rights which are identifiable through the exercise of human reason and which serve to define the basis and limits of legitimate political authority. Locke identified three such fundamental natural rights: rights to life, liberty, and property. Legitimate sovereign authority existed only to secure these rights, and securing these rights marked the limit of legitimate political authority. This has remained a central tenet of liberal political philosophy. Natural rights (in our terms, human rights) serve to impose a limit and constraint upon the exercise of political authority. The doctrine of natural rights provided a set of criteria for evaluating, criticising and, if necessary, taking action against one's political rulers. Rulers who failed to respect their subjects' natural rights could, ultimately, be condemned as illegitimate rulers who should be replaced with rulers who did respect these fundamental rights. To simplify two very complex historical events, this is precisely what happened during the American and French revolutions. At the level of ideological justification for violent revolutionary action, Britain's failure to respect the natural rights of the colonised and the French Ancien Régime's failure adequately to respect the rights of its subjects served to provide ostensive justification for action never before seen and established a historical precedent which continues to resonate today.

The principal focus of Locke's account of natural rights was individual liberty. While the terms of his appeal to natural rights implies attaching significant weight to the ideal of equality, Locke himself did not fully deliver such an argument. For this, we must turn to the writings of Jean-Jacques Rousseau (1968). Rousseau's contribution to the development of human rights is slightly coloured by his defence of the concept of the general will, which some have interpreted as a means for justifying authoritarian political rule (see Cranston, 1991). Leaving aside that particular debate, what Rousseau may be credited with is the formulation and development of an account of equality, required by an appeal to the notion that human beings possess rights by virtue of their humanity and not merely as a social privilege. Rousseau attributed to the state of nature a condition of equality between individuals, which social conventions and practices then usurped. The purpose of legitimate political rule was, in large part, to restore this condition of equality. The possession of natural rights thereby provides the means by which individuals may be both free and equal. In essence, the fundamental conceptual attributes of moral rights are thereby complete. They are universal and independent of any given social basis. They belong to individuals and provide the basis upon which the scope of legitimate political authority may be determined. Finally, they seek to provide for the exercise of freedom in accordance with reason, which, in principle at least, all individuals possess to an equal degree. In this form, moral rights provide the basis for determining what our legal rights ought to be in legitimate political states.

The concept of moral rights possesses a discernible historical development, emerging in the minds of thinkers and theologians and gradually seeking to establish an institutional embodiment in the doctrine of human rights. Given the limitations of approaching human rights in strictly legal terms, moral rights may be thought of as adding to the conceptual armoury of human rights advocates.

However, whilst it is clear that the myth of legal positivism cannot ultimately substantiate and justify a commitment to human rights, we still need to consider the strength of the justifications offered for moral rights.

As the discussion of the historical development of moral rights indicated, justifications for human rights as moral rights typically seek to establish a foundation beyond contingent social conditions. This involves distinguishing between existing moralities and justified (or enlightened) morality, whereby the latter provides the basis for determining the claims and authority of the former. James Nickel expresses the character of justified morality when he writes, 'a justified morality does not need to be accepted or practiced by anyone, nor does it necessarily have a social or institutional dimension' (1987: 39). On these terms, the legitimacy of a justified morality is not tied to its being tangibly or comprehensively recognised. The validity of justified moral principles is not conditional upon their being an established part of any human community or world-view. The truth of a justified morality is thereby to be located in human reason and a set of purportedly immutable conditions for a valued human existence. As we saw in the previous chapter, both interest and choice theories, in their respective ways, attempt to identify what such attributes may be. This approach to morality is, however, deeply problematic and controversial. There are two aspects to this which need concern us. The first concerns the claims being made for the basis and character of morality as a human institution. The second concerns the relatively obvious issue Nickel's definition raises for the efficacy of human rights based upon a 'justified' morality the authority of which is not based upon a sufficiently widespread recognition and acceptance of its terms. I shall consider each in turn.

Many contemporary attempts to identify the justified morality upon which human rights are based amount to a form of moral realism. Moral realism holds that the fabric of human reality necessarily contains normative truths (Nagel, 1986; Sayre-McCord, 1988). Moral realists argue that justified moral truths, or moral facts, simply do objectively exist for us as beings of a certain kind. Thus, Thomas Nagel (1986) argues that the suffering of a human being is simply and manifestly wrong. From this, he derives the conclusion that the morally correct thing to do is to prevent such suffering. Likewise, the taking of human life is simply wrong and cannot be condoned. Others may have contradictory and opposing views on these moral imperatives. An appeal to moral realism and the purported existence of moral facts enables those of us who are thinking correctly to point out the error of their opinions. Nagel's objective is not to justify human rights *per se*, but his formulation and defence of moral realism clearly have a close connection to the interest and choice theory approaches we considered in the previous chapter. The moral justification of human rights is best located in an appeal to some purportedly 'objective' and immutable moral facts. One task of human rights theorists is thus to seek to educate those whose moral opinions are not supported by the moral facts derived from an appeal to the tenets of moral realism. The letter, but more often the spirit, of moral realism has attracted significant critical attention in recent years, even amongst those who proclaim themselves to be advocates of human rights. Two examples will suffice to identify the grounds of this critique: Richard Rorty and Michael Ignatieff.

The philosophical basis of Rorty's critique of an appeal to the claim that human rights rest upon a moral realist foundation lies in an alternative approach to understanding moral claims and statements; emotivism. Emotivism must itself be located within the broader tradition of moral subjectivism, which stands fundamentally opposed to the moral realist claim that moral truths exist objectively and publicly for us. Moral subjectivism, in contrast, is based upon the claim that there are no such things as moral truths or moral facts (see Mackie, 1977). Moral subjectivism locates the origins of all moral commitments and beliefs as private subjective mental dispositions which distinct individuals come to hold through a variety of processes and mechanisms, but which, regardless of the manner in which they were acquired, remain inherently subjective. Traditionally, moral subjectivism sought to challenge appeals to 'objective' and substantive moral truths as binding upon all rational agents. It is interesting, therefore, to see its emotivist variant emerging amongst attempts nevertheless to justify a commitment to human rights.

Emotivist attempts to justify human rights take their bearings from a rejection of the claim that our moral beliefs and commitments can be ultimately based upon rational foundations. David Hume, the Eighteenth Century Scottish philosopher I have referred to before, provides a principal source and authority for this position. Emotivism argues that our moral commitments originate in our emotions and not our reason: morality is an affair of the heart and not the head. Thus, when an agent refers to something as morally good he or she is merely articulating an emotional disposition towards the thing in question. They are saying, in effect, that they like something and by expressing the agent's approval in the language of morals they are attempting, wittingly or unwittingly, to elicit other people's approval for the practice or phenomenon. To say that human rights are morally valid principles for regulating relations between individuals and public authorities is to express an emotional disposition towards – a liking for – human rights. It is important not to misconstrue emotivism on this point. One might conclude that emotivism merely relocates the source of a common human faculty for morality: from the head to the heart, so to speak. From this, it would still be perfectly possible to presume that the exercise of the moral faculty will still yield some commonality; that individuals' moral beliefs will still tend towards consensus and agreement. However, emotivism is not typically construed in these terms. Thus, so-called emotivist philosophers such as C.L. Stevenson (1944) and

Alasdair MacIntyre (1984) have explicitly argued that the subordination of the reasoning element in exercising a moral faculty results in significantly diverse and even contradictory moral beliefs and commitments. As with matters of taste and liking more generally, there are just different preferences and aversions: some people like things which others do not and vice versa. By insisting that all moral beliefs are based upon emotional dispositions, emotivism rules out the possibility of evaluating the relative strengths and weaknesses of different moral preferences. Emotivism denounces any attempt to judge different and competing moral beliefs by reference to purportedly rational criteria or forms of reasoning.

A contemporary exponent of emotivism is the American philosopher Richard Rorty. In his contribution to the 1993 Oxford Amnesty lectures, Rorty argued that, as a moral doctrine, human rights are not founded upon rational principles for the simple reason that no moral doctrine can ever be genuinely based upon rational foundations. Rorty insisted that this should not concern supporters of human rights. Human rights do not require theoretical underpinnings or complex intellectual journeys through unintelligible bodies of philosophical literature. Rorty argued that human rights require only that sufficient numbers of people are emotionally supportive of the doctrine: the heart is a more powerful force than the head. Having denied that there exist any objective moral facts, Rorty nevertheless proceeded to recommend human rights as a phenomenon which should be widely approved of. In particular, he argued that those who support human rights should seek to encourage their application through a form of sentimental education. For Rorty, the basis and efficacy of human rights derive not by appeal to a justified morality, in Nickel's terms, but from the diffusion of established and sufficiently practised sentiments.

Michael Ignatieff (2001) provides another example of an attempt to justify human rights at the explicit expense of an appeal to moral realism or purportedly rational moral foundations. While Ignatieff does not explicitly appeal to emotivist arguments in his critique and subsequent reformulation of human rights, he shares Rorty's insistence that the basis and efficacy of human rights must be based upon widespread and established practices and beliefs. Ignatieff argues that foundationalist philosophical attempts to justify human rights are doomed to failure as a consequence of the inherent contestability of all moral claims. He shares Rorty's rejection of any attempt to substantiate moral claims by appeal to moral facts or rational foundations. For his part, Ignatieff argues that the validity of human rights claims is a measure of the doctrine's political efficacy: the 'truth' of any human right is determined by its political effects and not by appeal to abstruse epistemological claims. He considers human rights to be inherently political and insists that practising human rights consists of the adoption of a distinct political position. To seek to promote and protect human rights is to be a participant in a political 'game'. Ignatieff presents this view of human rights as a corrective to what he refers to as 'human rights idolatory'. For him, far too many human rights defenders view what they do as being somehow 'pure' and untainted by partial, ideological interests. This leads to a form of unreflexive dogmatism and, more importantly for him, poor politics. Ignatieff insists that human rights are not above politics and are not free from ideological interests.[2] The presumption among human rights 'idolators' that their actions and commitments are justified by the objective moral fabric of human reality amounts to a politically motivated misunderstanding of the basis of the doctrine's authority. Despite this characterisation of human rights, Ignatieff insists that adhering to the 'human rights party' is a desirable political standpoint. Similarly, he also argues that the criterion for determining the justification of human rights claims is primarily founded upon the efficacy of the doctrine in realising its ends. Nickel's formulation of justified morality requiring few, if any followers, is thereby fundamentally rejected.

Rorty's account serves to challenge the manner in which morality is characterised by defenders of human rights as moral rights. In addition, Ignatieff offers an overt challenge to the view that the justification of moral rights is not conditional upon the extent to which they are accepted as objectively 'true', as moral facts. Taken together, these two critiques appear to offer a rebuttal to the argument that the existence and moral authority of human rights are not dependent upon their institutional embodiment, and a challenge to the claim that the legal recognition of human rights principles is neither necessary nor sufficient for their justified existence. While this need not lead us back to legal positivism, it does raise serious questions for the basis upon which a commitment to human rights may be established. Thus, some may be inclined to argue that a commitment to the moral authority of human rights rests upon an ability to demonstrate the legitimacy of a belief in the existence of publicly binding moral truths. On this view, the very legitimacy of human rights rests upon the veracity of moral realism and the existence of moral facts. To reject the latter is fundamentally to undermine the former. In their respective ways, both Rorty and Ignatieff aim to challenge this conclusion. After all, both assert their commitment to human rights despite their rejection of the type of approach which Nickel evokes in his notion of justified morality. The work of Rorty and Ignatieff suggests that it is possible to justify a commitment to human rights without necessarily endorsing a claim to moral truth. While neither advocates the primacy of law as the central mechanism for practising human rights, their work shares legal positivism's general scepticism of claims to moral truth.

---

[2]   I consider the political status of the human rights doctrine in greater detail in Chapter 7 when I discuss the alleged neutrality of human rights claims.

This may be initially appealing to some, especially those who have experienced nothing but frustration from engaging with moral philosophy. Like legal positivism, a justification for human rights might appear to be more effectively strengthened by appeals to their demonstrable existence and efficacy. Why expose one's faith in human rights to the apparent vagaries of moral reasoning when human rights principles already enjoy support and recognition? Many people do, it seems, feel human rights in their hearts, so to speak. Likewise, many people and institutions do recognise human rights in their political relationships. On this basis, we might better seek to justify human rights by reference to their existing recognition and influence. On this view, moral rights might be said to be victims of their own success in becoming politically and legally established. Thus, a need to justify human rights as moral rights existed prior to the emergence of what many have come to view as a wholesale and global human rights regime. The philosophical need for moral rights has thereby been superseded by the sheer extent of their institutionalisation as human rights. Rorty and Ignatieff might thereby be construed as offering a more 'realistic' and thus efficacious justification for human rights. Some supporters of human rights undoubtedly hold to this view and share a deep suspicion of arguments from the premise of moral facts. There are, however, very good reasons for rejecting the alternative positions outlined by Rorty and Ignatieff.

Rorty's espousal of an emotivist basis for and approach to human rights has attracted criticism from numerous quarters. Thus, Michael Freeman (2002) argues that justifications of human rights cannot dispense with an appeal to reasoning, as Rorty suggests. Defending human rights against their critics and opponents is not well served by simply insisting that such support just happens to *feel* right. Indeed, one would have to accept that one's own feelings were no more valid than those of one's opponent. One is left with a mere clash of different emotional constitutions. Those who are uncomfortable claiming that their own moral commitments are superior to others' may feel some sympathy with this scenario and may be tempted to reject Freeman's concerns. However, most who hold to this view also hold to a view about how best morally to regulate such disagreement. Many will propose some form of toleration or live and let live attitude. This is consistent with part of the *spirit* of human rights, but how is one to respond to circumstances where others reject this principle and insist that this is not a case of merely different moral beliefs co-existing but rather a conflict between false and valid beliefs, or even between good and evil beliefs? People such as these will reject the tolerance option. Justifying a commitment to a tolerant society will then require an appeal to reasons, rather than mere feelings. One can take this criticism of Rorty a step further. Rorty argues that feeling sympathetic towards human rights is a *good* thing. He insists that the more people who feel this way the better. However, Rorty's judgement and recommendation flagrantly contradict his dismissal of an appeal to criteria beyond mere sentiment and feelings. Rorty's liking for human rights is, on his terms, a mere liking and nothing more. There are no criteria beyond different emotions that will allow for distinguishing between better and worse emotions. Whilst Rorty's position does undoubtedly tap into an aspect of the current *Zeitgeist*, it suffers from too many fundamental weaknesses and contradictions to provide an adequate justification of human rights. Its apparent strength is derived from a frustration with an engagement with moral philosophy. Emotivism also offers an ostensibly credible explanation for why people tend towards disagreement, rather than agreement, when the topic concerns moral principles. However, unlike a strict legal positivist position, an emotivist justification of human rights appeals to morality as the basis for defending one's commitments. Its great flaw, however, lies in the inherent inability of emotivism to provide the kind of assured justification which Rorty still seeks to provide. What then of Ignatieff?

Ignatieff may be credited with raising a serious concern for our understanding of the theory and practice of human rights. He is, in my opinion, absolutely correct in describing human rights as political phenomena. Human rights are political. By this I do not mean that human rights comprise civil and political rights, which they do, but that to support human rights is to adopt a political position and will often entail a resort to political means in pursuit of one's human rights goals. It may be true to say that sometimes human rights defenders have been guilty of a certain form of moral righteousness which is not always very effective or even very appealing. However, saying that human rights should be understood as political phenomena does not mean that human rights are essentially and inherently political in character. This creates a similar problem for justifying one's commitment to human rights to the earlier approaches considered in this chapter. If human rights are inherently political then they are not qualitatively different from any other political position such as nationalism, authoritarianism or populism. Human rights become just one more *ism*. This approach confuses means with ends. Human rights may benefit from a greater recourse to political means, but this does not entail that the ends of human rights are therefore also essentially political. One may seek to pursue the defence of moral truths via political means, such as lobbying and campaigning, without diminishing the moral character of one's ends. Michael Freeman makes a similar point in his critique of the political approach to justifying human rights. Thus, he argues that the political approach to human rights attempts to exclude from human rights practice any notion of ideals or utopian visions on the ground that they do not help engage with the 'real world'. Freeman counters that ideals are fundamentally practical in so far as they provide criteria for evaluating social and political realities. He states, 'ideal theory directs us to the real possibilities that are worth realising' (2002: 57).

The political approach can therefore be criticised as failing to justify a commitment to human rights by conceding too much to social and political realities. The critical edge of human rights is thereby lost in an attempt to be (allegedly) better equipped for dealing with the cold light of day. In this sense, this approach bears a distinct similarity with the criticisms levelled earlier at legal-positivism. The essence of human rights comprises a capacity for criticising social, legal and political realities for their failure to adhere to the fundamental principles enshrined by a commitment to human rights. The doctrine must maintain a degree of independence from and critical engagement with distinct material conditions if it is to achieve its purpose. Justifying human rights requires appealing to moral principles which do not simply reduce to or wholly express the conditions which they must retain a capacity for critically evaluating. In their respective ways, legal positivism, emotivism and the political approach to human rights fundamentally jeopardise the critical independence of human rights.

Finally, both Rorty and Ignatieff exaggerate the depth and breadth of support for human rights in the world today. As I have indicated before, there has been a tendency towards assuming that the doctrine of human rights has become a veritable hegemonic power in regulating global geo-political relations. This is, quite simply, false and dangerously complacent. The true measure of the efficacy of human rights must be determined not by how many times their spirit is evoked, but by the systematic eradication of the abuse and violation of human rights. Even on the relatively modest criterion I defended in the previous chapter, we can say that all states abuse human rights; some do so some of the time and others do so much of the time. Some do so in violation of existing legal and political commitments and others do so in the absence of any such commitment. Too many human rights remain evident only on paper. Contrary to both Rorty's and Ignatieff's professed faith, the current geo-political reality does not adequately support a belief in the validity and efficacy of human rights. Given this, justifications for the doctrine must retain a degree of independence from the realities the doctrine seeks to influence and regulate.

STILL SEEKING A JUSTIFIED MORALITY

I have argued that the myth enshrined by the legal positivist approach to human rights is harmful to the doctrine through its inability to justify rights claims prior to or beyond the law. The counterpart to this view of human rights as legal rights is a defence of human rights as moral rights. However, the defence of moral rights is also problematic as a consequence of its debt to moral realism. Moral rights, despite their historical development, stand as veritable moral facts, thereby claiming to transcend contingent social conditions. While theorists such as Nickel insist that human rights can be justified only on this basis, other defenders of human rights argue that the doctrine may be justified without recourse to such potentially controversial and fragile claims. I have countered these alternative justifications of human rights and argued that they do not sufficiently allow for the maintenance of the critical independence of human rights from the social conditions they provide a moral means for evaluating. This claim, however, raises a number of other questions and concerns. Some of these will be addressed in the following chapter and my discussion of the social basis of human rights as a moral doctrine. What does need to be addressed here, however, is the question concerning the basis for identifying and defending human rights' critical independence.

Irrespective of the extent of their legal embodiment, human rights are inherently evaluative phenomena. They are concerned with identifying what the conditions are for each human being to enjoy the potential for leading a minimally good life. They grow out of an engagement with the form and content of human agency but do not merely reflect human reality *per se*. Rather, human rights offer an account of a basis in which a minimally good existence can be secured for all human beings. The realisation of human rights must overcome the stereotypical dualisms of friend and foe, insider and outsider, citizen and stateless person, and even, to some extent, the good and the bad. Realising human rights will require the establishment of a genuine commonality within an otherwise diverse and fragmented world. This is a truly formidable task and its accomplishment remains a distant aspiration. To this extent, human rights necessarily contain a 'utopian' element: pointing towards the realisation of conditions for the eradication of systematic human suffering and oppression, which are yet to be realised (see Orend, 2002). The utopian element of human rights is effectively synonymous with its stance of critical independence. However, like all other utopian projects, the human rights doctrine needs to justify itself in terms that are reasonable for all parties to accept. The justification of human rights as a moral doctrine which seeks legal and political recognition requires the identification of reasons for supporting human rights with words and actions. The essence of the doctrine – its appeal to humankind *per se* – renders this an extremely difficult task.

The way forward requires the identification of grounds for all having an overriding reason for supporting and respecting human rights. At present, these conditions do not exist, and morality provides an intellectually fragile place-holder for retaining a justification for the continuing attempt to realise the ambition of human rights. I argued in the previous chapter that Bryan Turner's attempt to justify human rights on the ground of mutual vulnerability was false to the extent that the world does not comply with his initial premise: some are far more vulnerable than others and the disparity reflects conditions which obstruct the rationale for a global commitment to human rights. Likewise, I argued that Gewirth's account of human rights as prerequisites for human agency was demonstrably false as stated, since much human life has proceeded without the protection of human rights. Neither of these approaches, in its current form, provides the grounds for a justified morality capable of substantiating a commitment to human rights in spite of, rather than because of, the shape of human realities. They both attempt to identify the grounds for human commonality, but ultimately provide unduly partial and restricted criteria. This should not, however, detract us from this intellectual course. Identifying the grounds of human commonality is essential to establishing the initial basis for the moral doctrine of human rights. I have argued elsewhere (Fagan, 2008) that preventing and overcoming systematic human suffering provides the fundamental moral imperative for a commitment to human rights. It would appear at the very least counter-intuitive to argue that no such imperative exists. We have sound reasons to seek to avoid systematic human suffering. While a focus upon suffering is essential, it is obviously only the initial ground for developing a justified account of which human rights we all have fundamental interests in enjoying. However, realising even this most general of moral aspirations remains a long way off. Developing this claim requires an engagement with the social reality of human rights and a detailed analysis of how it has interacted with other social and cultural realities. I have claimed that the search for the establishment of a justified morality capable of supporting a commitment to the ambition of human rights entails recognising the critically independent character of human rights so that they do not become mere hostages to fortune. Beyond this last reference to systematic human suffering, I have not offered an account of how this might be achieved, particularly in the face of a diverse and complex world. Chapter 3 aims to provide such an account.

3. Universalism and 'the other'

INTRODUCTION

Chapter 3 takes aim at a myth of moral universalism. This may seem surprising, if not somewhat perplexing, to some readers, given the tone and content of my argument in the previous two chapters. After all, I have suggested that justifying human rights requires a valid commitment to the existence of moral standards which are relatively 'modest' in scope, but which must nevertheless retain a degree of critical independence from the conditions to which many human beings are systematically exposed. A chapter devoted to critically analysing universalism would imply that I necessarily align myself with a form of moral relativism and that, in so doing, I effectively invalidate my argument to this point. A tendency to think in crudely dualistic terms, however, rarely does justice to the complexity of human affairs, and this is particularly the case when the concern is with human rights. This chapter does present a critical analysis of a certain form of universalism, whilst seeking to defend a moral commitment to ensuring that all human beings enjoy access to fundamental human rights. So, what then is the precise object of my concern and how does this chapter proceed?

Moral universalism has taken many forms. One may distinguish initially between secular and religious forms of universalism, or doctrines which lay claim to the title of universality. Without, at this point, identifying any particular manifestations of each it should be clear that the differing basis and content of each militate against the conclusion that both must be correct. Not all doctrines which lay claim to being universally valid actually are so. The particular approach to moral universalism which has, until relatively recently, been prevalent within the human rights doctrine is a complex amalgam of different secular and religious values and ideals. Despite its internal complexity, this account of moral universalism can be characterised as emphasising moral individualism at the expense of an alternative form of moral holism. It is also typically relatively unconcerned with the potentially constitutive properties of culture and society in the formation of ideals and values, including those which constitute its own outlook. Finally, based upon a faith in its adherence to moral individualism and a relatively asocial approach to human identity, this approach to moral universalism has tended to assume that the task which confronts human rights is the successful exporting of these purportedly asocial and universal values and ideals to the rest of the globe. While very few human rights theorists or practitioners speak overtly in these terms, the task may be characterised as the extension of the enlightenment project by the enlightened out towards the 'unenlightened' societies of the globe. It is this approach to human rights which, though very real, I am describing as based upon mythical presumptions about the human condition. It is also this approach to the promotion of human rights which I intend to analyse critically here.

The defence of human rights is bound to court controversy and attract criticism from those who have less of an immediate interest in the establishment of political orders devoid of systematic human rights abuse. It is possible that some advocates of human rights have too quickly dismissed criticism of their efforts as necessarily motivated by an aversion to the doctrine. This is regrettable. In recent years a growing body of thinkers and practitioners has begun to criticise the approach some have taken within the human rights community to those societies and cultures which do not immediately 'fit' the human rights social template. The nature of some of these societies and cultures is inherently oppressive and cannot be considered as sufficiently respectful of human rights in their current form. However, this does not mean that all societies whose moral fabric ostensibly differs from the values and ideals underlying human rights are similarly worthy of condemnation and attempts at conversion. A perceived tendency towards proselytising amongst some human rights advocates has attracted critical attention from some who are deeply sympathetic to the spirit of human rights but take issue with the approach some adopt towards the doctrine.

This critique of human rights proselytising is complex and cannot be reduced to a single perspective. There are, however, some recurring features which serve to orient my own discussion here. The first concerns a charge that the universalism on offer is actually anything but. That is to say, what is being presented as necessarily universal is actually a partial and localised perspective the relatively hegemonic influence of which owes more to military, political and, above all, economic power than the rational properties of the ideals and values in question. The second concerns the enduring tendency to misrepresent societal identity in crudely simplified terms, exemplified by categories such as the 'West' and the 'East', or more recently the 'North' and the 'South'. These terms tend to imply that the human rights project sits most easily within the one and requires a certain particular effort if it is to be successfully established in the other. The third follows on from the first two concerns insofar as this perspective is based upon a tendency to characterise people living beyond the 'natural' frontiers of human-rights-respecting societies as unduly recalcitrant or resistant to accepting the values and ideals 'we' have to offer: other societies become an 'other' for 'us', which is antithetical to the spirit of human rights whilst having influenced the doctrine's development. Finally, I discuss an alternative approach to moral universalism which seeks to avoid some of the overtly partial prejudices of this predominant understanding. This alternative account, however, takes very seriously and intends to avoid the moral inadequacies of an uncritical and unconditional form of moral relativism, which has been used all too often to seek to justify the continuing abuse of human rights.

DEFINING TERMS – UNIVERSALISM AND RELATIVISM

The theory of human rights has long been beset by the so-called universalism versus relativism debate (see Donnelly, 1985). In many respects, this debate has become a definitive landmark in the study of human rights. The implications of this debate are not, however, restricted to the realm of academia alone. How human rights are understood in the light of social complexity and difference is crucial to determining the scope of their application and the character of a legitimate relationship between human rights principles and existing social realities. It is, therefore, frustrating to learn that the various parties to this debate have all too often simply spoken past one another and have largely failed to establish a common understanding. This chapter aims to avoid this somewhat demoralising outcome, but in order to overcome the problem one must first understand its operative terms and concepts, beginning with the most fundamental: moral universalism and moral relativism.

The concept of moral universality holds that there exist universally valid and true principles and values. Universally valid and true principles and values are valid and true independently of social, political, economic, historical, religious, intellectual and cultural considerations and conditions. They aspire to be axiomatic in the sense that it is axiomatically true to say that 2+2 will always and everywhere equal 4. The importance of the universality principle for human rights was most recently reaffirmed in the 1993 Vienna Declaration, which boldly affirms the following: '[t]he World Conference on Human Rights reaffirms the solemn commitment of all states to confirm their obligations to promote universal respect for, and observance and protection of, all human rights and fundamental freedoms for all in accordance with the Charter of the UN ... The universal nature of these rights and freedoms is beyond question.'

While it does not spell out the content of the moral universalism being evoked, the Vienna Declaration provides a very clear and unequivocal example of human rights universalism. However, the Declaration proceeds to proclaim the following: '[w]elcoming the International Year of the World's

Indigenous People 1993 as a reaffirmation of the commitment of the international community to ensure their enjoyment of all human rights and fundamental freedoms and to respect the value and diversity of their cultures and
identities'.

Once again this appears sufficiently clear and reasonable. However, taken
together the two statements also serve to exemplify an operative tension
within the human rights community and its predominant conception of the
basis and social parameters of the doctrine. The tension derives from the
prescriptive character of the two statements and a descriptive analysis of actually existing societal cultures. On the face of it, the existence of societal
cultures the practices and values of which do not sufficiently comply with the
fundamental tenets of human rights prevents the possibility of human rights
advocates simply affirming the principle of respecting cultural diversity. A
commitment to the universal legitimacy of human rights is not consistent with
a commitment to the principle of respecting cultural diversity, since the former
entails a commitment to practices, values and ideals which may not necessarily exist within all societal cultures. Being judgemental of those human realities which do not comply with human rights principles is an unavoidable
feature of supporting human rights. The question is: what underlies this standpoint?

Typically, the account of moral universalism which has exerted the most
significant influence upon the development of human rights contains two
distinct characteristics: moral individualism and an account of human identity
which sets to one side the potentially constitutive features of societal cultures
upon human identity. I briefly consider each in turn.

Moral individualism holds to the claim that the only beings which possess
fundamental moral value are individual human beings. Each individual is
considered to be a distinct and inalienable bearer of abstract moral value, so
that each bearer of human rights is considered to be, in theory at least, a sovereign and separate moral entity. The influence of moral individualism upon the
human rights doctrine is apparent to the extent that the human rights doctrine
places the individual moral agent at the core of its principles. One consequence of this is the imposition of a normative restriction upon any public
authority's attempt to sacrifice an individual's or a minority group's rights and
interests in the name of the interests of the 'greater good'. As Ronald Dworkin
has consistently argued, an essential value of human rights claims consists of
the protection they offer to each and every individual. Each individual's
human rights are thereby considered to be non-aggregative and (in most cases,
at least),[1] cannot be overridden by aggregative calculations of overall utility.

---

[1]   Article 30 of the UDHR stipulates the categories of exceptions to this rule.

Dworkin thereby presents the power and function of rights claims as 'trump-ing' (or overriding) competing or alternative claims. Thus, from the human rights perspective, broadly defined, the relevant population of moral agents is construed as morally distinct and separate moral islands the claims of which are not conditional upon calculations of collective or aggregative welfare. Human rights characterise the individual as a morally sovereign entity.

In keeping with the moral status accorded to the individual, the human rights doctrine has also been significantly influenced by a perspective upon the basis or sources of human moral identity. The form of moral universalism which has most influenced human rights has traditionally adopted what may be referred to as an asocial approach to human moral identity, which subordi-nates or rejects the potential influence of social conditions upon a morally universalist perspective and the constitution of moral reasoning. The natural rights tradition exemplifies this approach, given its stress upon the existence of moral principles which precede any specific social formation. Similarly, Kant's moral philosophy shares this commitment to construct a veritable moral universe out of the identification of purportedly pure forms of reason. Both of these approaches have significantly influenced the development of a perspective which views society as non-essential in the formation of moral reasoning and the identification of human beings' moral identity and commit-ments. This asocial perspective complements the emphasis accorded to the moral sovereignty of the individual. Furthermore, both components of this account of moral universalism underlie a further assumption that the substan-tive moral commitments they yield are themselves necessarily universal and irreducible to any particular social or political doctrine.

The conventional counterpart to moral universalism is moral relativism. Moral relativism is an established perspective upon the sources and status of moral reasoning and beliefs. It has been defined in the following terms: 'moral relativism ... often takes the form of a denial that any single moral code has universal validity, and an assertion that moral truth and justifiability, if there are such things, are in some way relative to factors that are culturally and historically contingent' (Wong, 1991: 442). Moral relativism rejects the claim that there can exist moral principles and forms of moral identity which are not themselves determined by social and cultural conditions: morality reflects distinct social forms. Moral relativism has sometimes been confused with other positions, most notably nihilism. Nihilists argue that morality has lost its authority and ability legitimately to command our rational compliance with moral dictates: nihilists view morality as a chimera. In contrast, relativists do not deny either the existence or the potential efficacy of morality. They do deny the legitimacy of purportedly universal moral doctrines, but they do not thereby consider morality to be a purely arbitrary or random affair. A relativist will typically argue that morality does exist, or rather that different moralities exist across time and space. The common origin of these moralities is culture, or society. Cultures and societies have differed and do differ fundamentally, and this is reflected in the existence of a bewildering range of different moral beliefs and customs. Morality is determined by society and there is not (empirically speaking) a common, entirely agreed-upon moral code for all existing societies. What is morally permissible in Toronto may be morally taboo in Tehran. Likewise, something which is morally condemned in London may be perfectly acceptable in Lahore or Lusaka.

A careful reading of the above will detect that two potentially distinct elements are being run together in this formulation of relativism. It is, therefore, important to distinguish between two manifestations or depictions of relativism: descriptive relativism and prescriptive relativism (Nickel, 1987). Descriptive relativism consists of an empirical claim that moral beliefs, values and practices do fundamentally differ across time and place. These differences are so incommensurable, it is claimed, as to prevent the identification of any single moral code adhered to by all human beings. Descriptive relativism was clearly apparent in the draft statement on the universal rights of man prepared by the American Anthropological Association in its denunciation of a social basis for moral universalism. It has also been expressed through the work of Ruth Benedict (1935) and more recently Alison Dundes Renteln (1988). While descriptive relativism consists of an empirical sociological claim, prescriptive relativism appeals more overtly to philosophical argument in its opposition to moral universalism. Prescriptive relativism extends relativism beyond the empirical realm and offers a distinctly favourable evaluation of moral diversity. Prescriptive relativism contains two elements: 'negative' and 'positive'. The negative element owes much to the moral subjectivism we considered in the previous chapter in its denial of the very possibility of morality yielding and comprising universally valid moral facts. The 'proper' exercise of human morality, it is claimed, yields diverse and even incommensurate moral beliefs and practices. Morality offers no Archimedean point from which universal and immutable moral truths may be identified. The positive element takes relativism much further and offers an evaluative argument in support of fundamental diversity. This positive approach argues that moral diversity is itself to be approved of. On this view, it is a morally good thing that there can exist no single and valid moral code for all human beings everywhere.

The general conceptual features of universalism and relativism should now be sufficiently clear for one to be able to analyse their effects upon and presence within the theory and practice of human rights. Human rights is a universal doctrine. This is beyond reasonable question. The issue, of course, concerns precisely what form this universalism may legitimately take in order to realise the ambition of human rights. This will become clearer throughout this chapter. Viewing human rights as a universal doctrine provides an initial and clear indication of the contribution relativism can make to human rights. Human rights are based upon a universalist foundation; relativism rejects the legitimacy of any such foundation. Therefore, one cannot be both a relativist and a human rights supporter. They are fundamentally incompatible with one another. This does not mean that human rights supporters must necessarily be insensitive to cultural diversity (although the next section discusses the allegation that many have been insensitive to other societal cultures). Nor does it mean that relativists are morally impoverished people. But it does mean that a true relativist cannot also be a true human rights supporter. Simply pointing to the incompatibility between human rights and relativism does not suffice to establish the inadequacies of the latter. In this respect, relativism may be criticised on three distinct grounds.

The initial ground of criticism concerns the implications of the possible truth of relativism for human rights. If there really were no common moral grounds for consensus and agreement the human rights doctrine simply could not legitimately exist. The truth of relativism would demonstrate the moral illegitimacy of human rights. In itself, this is not a particularly strong criticism. As the philosopher Friedrich Nietzsche (1967) famously argued, we cannot establish the truth of something by pointing to the potentially adverse consequences of its not being true: the truth does not always yield favourable outcomes. The second ground of criticism concerns the validity of the descriptive claim being made by relativists. The discourse of human rights has suffered from its fair share of inflated rhetoric and grandiose claims. I have argued earlier that there are good reasons to challenge the claim that we live in an age of human rights, or that human rights possess a hegemonic influence upon geopolitical affairs. Human rights are not universally established and practised. This may appear to lend weight to the descriptive thesis. However, we should hesitate before assuming that the descriptive thesis rests upon the secure evidential base which its advocates assume. There is no global survey of moral practices and customs. There has been no rigorous and methodologically robust study of what human communities hold to be morally legitimate. There is undoubtedly ethnographic evidence of diverse moral practices and customs, but this cannot provide a thoroughly comprehensive account of the empirical character of human morality. All too often, relativists assume that simply pointing to some moral diversity will suffice to establish the truth of relativism. This is ultimately poor scholarship. Set against this, we must consider the possibility that, empirically speaking, there are some fundamental and recurring moral commitments found across a wide range of societal cultures. Thus, a belief in variously formulated conceptions of human dignity presents itself as a moral commitment that is widely adhered to. Similarly, a belief in the wrongness of taking innocent human life appears to be a recurring motif of many moral belief systems. Finally, the very existence of human rights as a universal moral doctrine must be considered as evidence which contradicts the descriptive relativist claim. Human rights are not protected everywhere, but there is a very widespread belief in their general moral value and in the moral necessity of establishing a global regime of adequate respect for human rights. Taken together, these forms of counter-evidence do not serve categorically to refute relativism, but they do provide evidence which relativists typically ignore or fail to account for.

The final ground for criticising relativism concerns its prescriptive variant. Put simply, prescriptive relativism is essentially incoherent and founders upon a basic contradiction. Recommending relativism as a morally valuable good for all societal cultures is unequivocally a universalist claim. It is a claim which cannot be extrapolated from the content of existing moral belief systems either, since many such belief systems are fully committed to the presumed superiority of their own particular version of moral truth. There is thus no intellectual or empirical basis for the normative assertion that relativism is a universally legitimate moral doctrine. Many prescriptive relativists appear to misconstrue themselves for something that they are not. What they actually recommend is a form of toleration, which takes various forms (Mendus, 1988) but the essence of which consists of a claim that there are many different paths to achieving a morally good life and societal culture, and a proper understanding of moral universalism allows for both the legitimate making of this claim and a comprehensive degree of moral diversity. In effect, some prescriptive relativists should better be understood as moral pluralists, a doctrine which I shall consider in due course but which has rather different implications for human rights' relationship with moral diversity than the prescriptive relativist assertion would allow for.

Given the collected limitations of relativism and the clearly universalist character of an appeal to human rights as moral goods which all human beings should enjoy sufficient access to, it appears perfectly reasonable to conclude that human rights is best understood as a universalist moral doctrine. This conclusion, however, raises several highly significant questions. Does the falsity of relativism absolve human rights from all subsequent moral criticism? To what extent can the doctrine of human rights be understood as indebted to distinct social and cultural influences? Finally, what implications do the answers to these two questions hold for understanding the universality of human rights claims?

ETHNOCENTRICITY AND HUMAN RIGHTS

The mere fact of a moral doctrine's universality does not, of course, serve to validate the specific claims and commitments which comprise the doctrine. Christianity is a universal doctrine, as is Islam. Both claim to have identified the basis and content of universal moral truth. Neither doctrine, needless to say, actually enjoys universal support and affirmation. In this respect, the human rights doctrine appears to have been rather more successful in eliciting support than its overtly religious counterparts. This has not, however, absolved human rights from attracting a vein of criticism more commonly levelled at religious doctrines in their attempts to attract followers and converts. The essence of this criticism is that the human rights doctrine suffers from a degree of conceptual and practical ethnocentrism, which serves significantly to restrict the doctrine's legitimate application within a complex and diverse world. This criticism is levelled by those who are sympathetic and those who are hostile to human rights' claims to universality. The criticism is also levelled by thinkers from a diverse range of cultures and ideological backgrounds. Before we consider examples of these, it is important to be clear about what ethnocentricity consists of.

The Oxford English Dictionary defines 'ethnocentricity' in the following terms: 'centred on one's race or ethnic group; based on or characterised by a tendency to evaluate other races or groups by criteria specific to one's own; having assumptions or preconceptions originating in the standards, customs, etc., of one's own race or group'. The ethnocentric character of human rights would, therefore, consist of the attempted application of culturally partial values and ideals upon the rest of the world's cultures. The charge of ethno-centricity would also imply a view that such values and ideals must them-selves have distinct cultural origins which serve to restrict their application to similar cultural contexts and invalidate attempts to over-extend their applica-tion. Human rights have been criticised on precisely these grounds. Interestingly, they have been criticised by those who ostensibly might appear to inhabit a cultural context most closely associated with the origin of human rights: Anglo-American and western European societal cultures. Thus, the political scientists Pollis and Schwab (2000) have argued that the legitimate application of human rights is restricted by their principally and characteristi-cally 'western' origins and development. On this view, human rights may 'belong' to the West but are largely incapable of metaphorically travelling beyond the frontiers of western civilisations. Similarly, Samuel Huntington (1996) has insisted that human rights belong exclusively to the West and that a geo-politics based upon a presumption that human rights can be effectively established across the world is doomed to failure. Outside 'western' societies, other thinkers have also argued that the legitimate application of human rights is severely restricted by the doctrine's alleged failure to acknowledge the extent to which the doctrine is based upon unduly partial and parochial values and ideals. The African writer Issa Shivji (1989) has denounced human rights as a latter-day attempt to convert and colonise Africa to a set of western values which are ultimately incompatible with African belief systems. A somewhat more sympathetic African appraisal of human rights has been developed by the political philosopher Makau Mutua (2002). Whilst he does seek to develop an account of human rights which is capable of securing normative legitimacy for Africans, Mutua criticises the conventional approach to human rights as unduly ethnocentric. He writes, 'as currently constituted and deployed, the human rights movement will ultimately fail because it is perceived as an alien ideology in non-Western societies' (2002: 14). Beyond America, Europe and Africa human rights have also attracted criticism from supporters of Islam and from within 'Asia' more generally (see An-Na'im, 1992). The recurring focus of concern for 'non-western' critics consists in the importance placed upon the moral sovereignty of the individual and a corresponding diminution in collective and cultural moral values in determining people's lives. From this perspective, human rights are criticised for unduly reflecting a partial social and political experience most closely associated with the development of liberal-democratic legal and political systems in North America and Europe.

The charge levelled at human rights is serious and requires an extended engagement. If it is true to say that human rights are unduly ethnocentric then we should expect this to have potentially devastating effects upon the doctrine's long-term legitimacy. It would create (or help to explain) a clear and recurring problem for the implementation of some human rights principles as an allegedly common standard for all peoples everywhere. Indeed, from this perspective even those broadly sympathetic to the spirit of human rights are liable to view the doctrine as a form of cultural imperialism which is, at worst, oblivious to, at best, insensitive towards actual cultural and social practices and customs. On this view, human rights are accused of being a partial western moral doctrine the global application of which is facilitated not by the authority of moral truth but by the political and economic influence of 'western' geo-political powers. On this view, human rights cannot adequately assimilate a sufficient respect for cultural diversity, but represent a stick to beat non-compliant societies and cultures with. The effects of this view have fed through to even the established institutions of the legal human rights regime. Thus, practical examples of individual nation-states resorting to this kind of argument can be found in the relatively large number of reservations made against the implementation of CEDAW, on the ground that some aspects of CEDAW were culturally insensitive. Michael Freeman (2002: 104) notes the specific example of Saudi Arabia objecting to the UDHR's enshrined right to marry as applying to freely consenting parties. Similarly, the Cairo Declaration frames rights to religious practice in terms which accord particular significance to Islam. Finally, the African Charter of Human Rights highlights the importance of collective moral goods for Africa in its appeal to the

rights of human beings and 'people'. Taken together, both the theoretical criticisms of the cultural character of human rights and the institutional amendments to the human rights doctrine are based upon an explicit or implicit
allegation that human rights have become unduly reflective of a partial
cultural experience. The ethnocentricity of human rights consists of an inability or reluctance to recognise the partial cultural influences upon the substance
of the doctrine and, finally, this either serves fundamentally to invalidate the
doctrine's application beyond its 'natural' cultural context, or justifies entering
significant reservations against or amendments to the international legal
human rights regime.

Applying the allegation that human rights suffer from a degree of ethnocentricity to the theory and practice of human rights entails a number of potentially adverse consequences. Particularly significant is the accompanying
implication that the ethnocentricity of human rights will result in non-western
societies being attributed a character of 'otherness' to allegedly human rights
supporting societies. As Edward Said (1978) has argued, American and
European political and cultural hegemony has been pursued, in part, through a
cultural project which seeks to underline a sense of western moral superiority
by representing non-western civilisations in morally and culturally diminished
terms: other cultures are judged in the light of purportedly universal criteria
(which are actually only idealisations of western civilisation) and are found
wanting in respect of their inability fully to comply with 'our' idealised standards. This process and outcome are, ultimately, determined by the possession
and exercise of power and have little to do with 'objectively' valid and legitimate criteria. If the charge of ethnocentrism sticks to human rights, all of the
doctrine's supporters have very real cause for concern. This is, then, part of
what is at stake in this particular debate. How, though, can the charge of ethnocentrism be evaluated?

We should begin by distinguishing between those critics whose motive is
sympathetic to the spirit of human rights and those whose criticism appears
motivated by far more partial interests. Thus, former East Asian political leaders, such as Mahatir Mohammed and Lee Kwan Yew, have consistently characterised human rights as being fundamentally incompatible with so-called
Asian values (see Chan, 1999; Donnelly, 1999). During their tenure both leaders were criticised inside and outside 'Asia' for their poor human rights
records. As Chan (1999) has argued, there is nothing distinctively and legitimately 'Asian' about political despotism and oppression. While this approach
may appear to load the dice in favour of a commitment to human rights, I do
not think attempted rationalisations of political oppression should be accorded
much intellectual weight here. Setting aside those whose motives may reasonably be assumed to be somewhat nefarious, we are left with two possible
responses to the charge of ethnocentrism. The charge can be either denied or

accepted. I turn now to consider those who deny the charge, before I engage with the detail of those who, though sympathetic to human rights, accept the charge.

One way of addressing this issue is to ask, as Heiner Bielefeldt (2000: 99) has done, whether human rights emerge out of the 'cultural genes' of the West. Bielefeldt's focus concerns the relationship between human rights and Islam, and he concludes that human rights are not unduly restricted by an undeniable affinity with their western cultural origins and development. In effect, Bielefeldt denies the charge of ethnocentricity. Another theorist who provides a far more detailed denial of the charge is Jack Donnelly (2002). Like Bielefeldt, Donnelly accepts the historical facts of the primarily western origins and development of human rights. He also insists that these origins have no effective or necessary bearing upon the legitimate scope of the doctrine. In effect, Donnelly accuses those who present the origins of human rights as serving to limit their legitimate geographical scope as falling foul of the so-called genetic fallacy; a false conclusion drawn from a true premise, that the 'birth place' of any moral or political doctrine necessarily determines the restricted scope of its valid application. Donnelly argues that human rights should better be understood not in culturally essentialist terms but in structural terms.

Donnelly repeats a conventional academic assumption that human rights are closely tied to what has come to be referred to as 'modernity'. In actuality modernity refers to a deeply complex and convoluted amalgam of material and normative phenomena (see Blumenberg, 1983). Typically, modernity is associated with the establishment of democratic political systems, the rule of law, the formal liberty and equality of individuals, the establishment of a functioning civil society and the secularisation of political authority. More controversially, some also associate modernity with the establishment of relatively free economic markets. For his part, Donnelly selects the rise of the modern nation-state, the establishment of free markets and the rise of political claims to equality and toleration as the principal structural characteristics of modernity. Donnelly insists, against the prevailing natural rights perspective, that human rights are not based upon timeless and immutable moral constructs. Rather, he views human rights as distinct socio-historical phenomena: moral and legal constructs tied to the development of the principal structural characteristics of modernity. Whilst these characteristics emerge in the West the forces of globalisation have, in effect, exported and recreated these conditions across an ever-widening swathe of the globe. Quite independently, then, of the persistence of indigenous or traditional belief systems, human rights have emerged as the necessary normative correlates of the structural forces of an increasingly globalised modernity. Donnelly's general thesis has received support from others working on more specific and localised aspects of the development of human rights. Thus, Rhoda Howard (1986) views the development of human rights in Africa through a similarly social-structural lens. Howard rejects claims by some Africans that the application of human rights in Africa should be conditional upon their compatibility with indigenous and traditional African customs and beliefs. In effect, Howard denies that any such traditional phenomena continue to exert any actual or significant influence upon commonwealth African societies. In effect, she claims that commonwealth Africa has been increasingly assimilated within a globalised geo-political and economic system, characterised by the predominance of the nation-state and the emergence of relatively free economic markets. Claims to authentic African traditions, she insists, are almost always made by those political elites who seek only to protect and expand their political power. She states, 'most assertions of cultural relativity in fact are an ideological tool to serve the interests of powerful emergent groups in commonwealth African societies' (1986: 17). Africa has become, as a consequence of its exposure to the West, very much more structurally western in character than claims to indigenous authenticity could ever acknowledge. Human rights exist to protect individuals against certain structural forces, and these forces are alive and well in Africa and necessitate the establishment of an effective human rights regime.

Both Donnelly and Howard reject the view that recognisable precedents for human rights are identifiable in many non-western traditions. Donnelly, however, explicitly insists that this is due purely to structural and not essentially cultural factors. He is not, thereby, seeking ethnocentrically to condemn non-western societies for failing to conform to 'our' morally superior ideals and values. Indeed, any structuralist argument necessarily militates against claims to cultural essentialism or the cultural genes, which Bielefeldt refers to. Neither is Donnelly seeking to claim that human rights provide the definitive or sole criteria for morally valuable beliefs and perspectives. He acknowledges, for example, that most (if not all) cultures have possessed notions of human wellbeing and flourishing. Thus, most religions possess a clear concept of human dignity. However, Donnelly argues that these should not be seen as embryonic or prototypical normative manifestations of human rights. While the ideal of human dignity obviously has an important role to play in the basis of human rights as a moral doctrine, the scope of human rights extends very much further than such concerns. Human rights possess a specific and distinct character of their own, which is largely determined by the function they are required to play in modern societies. The depth and breadth of these functions are themselves determined by the distinct and specific character of the structural forces and components of modern societies. The need for human rights is, thus, primarily structural, rather than entirely moral. Furthermore, the extent to which these structural needs have been spread throughout the world provides the ultimate justification for their existence and a simultaneous refutation of the charge of ethnocentricity. Human rights may have emerged in a distinct time and place, but they did so in response to circumstances which everyone now faces. The alleged partiality of human rights norms is refuted by the fact of everyone's comparable need for them. Donnelly concludes this account of human rights with an assertion which counters the allegedly limited appeal of human rights and states, 'in all regions of the world, a strong commitment to human rights is almost universally accepted' (2002: 91). He accepts that a degree of cultural variability exists in respect of the interpretation and form given to fundamental human rights concepts in some parts of the world, but concludes that this does not extend, or amount to, a challenge to the very basis of the human rights doctrine. Finally, in contrast to the assumption upon which the ethnocentric charge is founded, Donnelly asserts that 'there are authoritative international human rights norms ... The standards of internationally recognized human rights are minimal standards of decency, not luxuries of the West' (2002: 159).

An alternative rejection of the charge of ethnocentricity can be discerned in the work of Alan Gewirth, whose account of human rights we have already encountered. By way of reminder, Gewirth locates the necessity for human rights in the very prerequisites for human agency: all human agents have a similar, if not entirely equal, interest in the possession of human rights, and human rights are not so much things one exercises, but the means by which one can enjoy agency *per se*. Gewirth has developed his initial account in an explicit attempt to address some of the criticisms levelled at him in respect of the theory's apparent disregard for the political context in which rights may be possessed. Thus, in his *The Community of Rights* (1996) Gewirth acknowledges the necessity of political community for developing and claiming fundamental human rights. However, he does not see the establishment of an appropriate political community as determinative of the basis for and justification of human rights. Ultimately, human rights adhere to all agents, irrespective of the particular political institutions to which they are exposed. This is obviously very different from Donnelly's approach outlined above. Where Donnelly views the development of particular institutions as preceding and determinative of the development of human rights, Gewirth's argument tying them into the prerequisites for human agency effectively turns Donnelly's argument on its head, and insists that institutions develop in the light of the moral imperative of human rights as essential, rather than merely contingent, elements of human agency. Gewirth's account shares Donnelly's rejection of the charge of ethnocentricity. Some parts of the world may well be more effective at ensuring the protection of human rights, but this does not mean that rights somehow belong to specific regions. Nor, given their apparent necessity for human agency, does it mean that only agents in those parts of the world can be said to enjoy a culturally 'genuine' or authentic relationship with human rights. Human rights, as the term suggests, belong to all human beings to an equal degree. Ultimately, the charge of ethnocentricity is guilty of the genetic fallacy, falsely views human rights as determined by the alleged *genetic genes* of the West, falsely denies the actual need human beings have for human rights, either in the collective and shared exposure to modernity, or as basic attributes of human agency. Finally, the charge of ethnocentricity is all too often levelled by those who have a perceived interest in forestalling the empowering spread of human rights.

I have, of course, sought to exclude the latter from my account of the potentially ethnocentric character of some part of either the theory or the practice of the latter. The nefariously motivated critics do not, however, exhaust the constituency of those who, though sympathetic to the ambition of human rights, have real concerns primarily about the means by which some human rights supporters have sought to achieve their ends. To a lesser extent, there are also questions to be asked about precisely how the ends of human rights are understood; what they substantively consist of and entitle individuals to. Returning more overtly to the subject of this chapter, both Donnelly's and Gewirth's respective accounts of human rights effectively exclude the possibility of the myth I am countering arising. Some human rights advocates might be occasionally guilty of a somewhat zealous approach to the doctrine, perhaps, but the problem of proselytising does not arise for the simple reason that the world's populations are, it is claimed, already converted, either by exposure to globalising modernity or by a proper understanding of the necessity of human rights for human agency. In respect of Gewirth's arguments, I refer the reader to my earlier criticisms of his particular brand of choice theory. In respect of Donnelly's claims, rather more can be usefully said at this point.

The debate surrounding the cultural context and character of human rights in the modern world suffers from a surfeit of cultural essentialism. Contributors to the debate speak of the 'West' and the 'East' or 'Asia' and 'Africa' as if these terms were not so much convenient shorthand for complex cultural phenomena but actually existing discrete entities. This is, of course, utter nonsense. As singular, discrete entities, there are no such things as the 'West' and the like. This is crucially important to understanding how an account of human rights may be developed which is not unduly in thrall to a purportedly single geo-political and cultural bloc. Likewise, one may challenge the vision of modernity which typically accompanies claims that the West (either as a cultural entity or the source of a set of structural phenomena) is largely responsible for developing and expounding the human rights doctrine. While this is absent from Donnelly's account, others have implied by this that the West and modernity may lay claim to a certain degree of moral superiority and hence justified authority. It is this latter allusion that many legitimate critics of human rights proselytising are suspicious of, given their typically rather different experience of modernity and western civilisation. This latter is also deeply relevant to Donnelly's vision although any engagement with it is almost entirely absent from his account.

As I have argued earlier, the modern human rights movement emerges as a response to the Holocaust, a distinctly 'European' phenomenon, which utilised the forces of scientific technology and state bureaucracy (both central elements of modernity) systematically to annihilate millions of people. In addition, while slavery was an established practice in many parts of the world, it took European 'ingenuity' and commitment to turn the practice into a vast economy built quite literally on the backs of millions of Africans' suffering and death. One can also add the effects of various European empires upon swathes of the globe to the litany of European-induced human suffering and oppression. Lest anyone imagine that these are purely historical phenomena, we must also consider the effects of the global inequality of wealth, which benefits the few at the expense of the lives and deaths of the many. One may also add to this the terrible plight of indigenous peoples in North America and Australasia in the face of the modern societies which have stolen land and denied the reproduction of cultural traditions. Modernity has an ocean of blood on its hands (see Horkheimer and Adorno, 1973). Those spilling the blood have been typically of European descent, whilst those whose blood is spilt have been all too often non-Europeans or perceived 'others' to the development of European or North American civilisation. It is truly astonishing how little is actually written about these demonstrable facts in accounts of human rights' 'western' heritage. Genocide, imperial oppression, slavery, gross economic inequalities in global wealth and the destruction of indigenous peoples are no more distinctive characteristics of an essentialised 'West' than respect for human rights, the rule of law and the consolidation of democratic institutions are, but they are vitally important components for developing a sufficiently accurate and objective account of 'us'. They are also vital to understanding why some have remained suspicious of human rights and fear the doctrine as yet another conceited export from civilisations which have all too often failed to practise what they have preached to others and in the light of which these others have been found morally wanting and legitimate objects of concern.

In understanding the basis and motive for the arguments developed by those who, though sympathetic to the ambition of human rights, have nevertheless criticised some approaches to human rights as unduly ethnocentric in character it is important to see that the West is not always and by everyone perceived as humanity's 'saviour'. The saviour/victim relationship affects a great deal of political discourse and humanitarian rhetoric. It is also a clearly established feature of the human rights discourse. However, it harbours numerous dangers. One such consists of the ultimately false and conceited view that the West may be characterised in relatively morally pure terms as a would-be global saviour. In actuality, the effects of a very great deal of western political, economic and military action have been truly devastating and have provided a principal motive for the need for human rights in order to protect peoples from western policies and actions. Failing to acknowledge and understand this fact constitutes a significant and very damaging omission on the part of some human rights supporters, theorists and practitioners alike. In pursuing this line of argument, it is also critical to acknowledge that human rights do not exclusively belong to the West and nor does everything the West has practised and affirmed amount to a form of respect for human rights. It is important not to reproduce the very cultural essentialism and political naïvety one has overtly criticised to this point. There have been several attempts to produce an account of human rights in the light of an awareness of the danger of ethnocentricity. I shall focus upon two found in the work of Makau Mutua and John Rawls.

ATTEMPTING TO AVOID ETHNOCENTRICITY

Mutua (2002) has sought to avoid reproducing ethnocentric prejudices in his approach to human rights in Africa. From this basis he has sought to develop a universal account of human rights which is not unduly restricted by singular cultural influences. In essence, Mutua has developed what may be referred to as an ecumenical approach to human rights. As the title suggests, an ecumenical approach seeks harmoniously to assimilate and combine a number of different cultural and religious elements in reconstructing a new understanding of the basis and scope of human rights. The particular object of his concern is what he considers to be the undue emphasis placed upon moral individualism within the conventional human rights doctrine. Put simply, he argues that not all cultures and religions share this particular ideal. In actual fact, the majority of cultures and religions adopt a more collectivist or holist approach to conceptualising moral communities. An insistence upon defending and expounding overtly individualist values and ideals will, he insists, serve to undermine the legitimacy of human rights for many peoples across the globe. He also proceeds to argue that the status of individualism within the conventional human rights doctrine provides a criterion by which some human rights supporters have perjoratively evaluated other cultures: a rhetorical espousal of individualism provides the basis for determining between human rights supporting and human rights violating cultures and societies. He also insists that the West has all too often both disregarded the devastating effects of its interventions in non-western societies and simply assumed that such societies are incapable of saving themselves. Human rights becomes a kind of 'white man's burden' for the modern age. Finally, Mutua argues that human rights are too closely associated with a distinct and particularly liberal political paradigm. He argues that not all societies share a commitment to liberalism and those which do not are not necessarily thereby illegitimate: liberalism does not enjoy a monopoly upon claims to political legitimacy.

In attempting to reconstruct an ecumenical approach to human rights Mutua insists that a commitment to moral individualism is not essential or necessary for the doctrine. He also insists that the human rights doctrine need not have a singular and essential identity that is everywhere and anywhere the same and unchanging. To this extent, some degree of cultural variability is allowed for beyond that allowed for by liberalism. However, he insists that what form these take must be determined by the people to whom the doctrine is applied. What human rights are in any part of the world cannot simply be determined by existing political élites and power-holders but must be determined from the 'bottom up' and thus by ordinary people. This element is thereby presented as essential for legitimising both the process and the outcome of determining which human rights should be adhered to and secured. To complete this alternative account of human rights, he argues that the common element of human rights may be discerned in the concept of human dignity. The fundamental object of human rights should be securing the necessary conditions for human dignity. The universality of this function is secured by the universality of the concept of human dignity. He insists that all cultures and societies include and accord fundamental significance to this ideal, which, though it may vary across time and place, retains common elements in the distinction it draws between the moral value of human beings and other species and a commitment to a recurring vision of moral absolutes, such as the wrongness of taking innocent life and inflicting unnecessary suffering.

In conclusion, Mutua insists that such alternative or indigenous accounts of human rights must be developed if the doctrine is not to become even more widely perceived by ordinary non-westerners as a culturally alien imposition. A commitment to human rights must not become synonymous with a mere proselytising of partial values and ideals. If the ambition of human rights is to be realised, the doctrine must not be perceived as a mere attempt to universalise and morally legitimise a set of partial and unduly parochial cultural values and ideals. An ecumenical approach is required if human rights is to overcome the ethnocentric slur. In Mutua's own words, this ecumenical approach will require that 'the cultures and traditions of the world must, in effect, compare notes, negotiate positions, and come to agreement over what constitutes human rights. Even after agreement, the doors must remain open for further inquiry, reformulation and revision' (2002: 74).

For his part, John Rawls's work is not exemplified by a concern for any alleged ethnocentricity within the human rights doctrine. Rawls sought to develop a broader account of justice within modern domestic and international political systems which encompassed an account of human rights. It would also be fair to say that Rawls's formulation of just political principles developed from an initially somewhat Kantian perspective presented in his *Theory of Justice* (1971) into a somewhat more pragmatist vision expounded in his later *Political Liberalism* (1993). Despite their substantive differences, both of these works sought to address the domestic, national context of a broadly constitutionally democratic political system. A Rawlsian account of international justice and the significance of human rights for a just global order was only finally presented in his *The Law of Peoples* (1999), which provides the focal point of my analysis of his account of human rights.

Three elements are particularly important to understanding Rawls's approach to human rights as expounded in *The Law of Peoples*. First, Rawls acknowledges that liberalism as a comprehensive account of moral goodness is not capable of securing universal rational validity. He considers comprehensive liberalism to be merely one of a number of very different moral conceptions of the good present in the world today. Second, he argues that a commitment to reciprocity is essential to developing a legitimate account of global justice within a complex and culturally diverse world. His focus upon the ideal of reciprocity seeks explicitly to forestall the effects of the unequal distribution of power and influence. He writes, 'when terms are proposed as the most reasonable terms of fair cooperation, those proposing them must think it at least reasonable for others to accept them as free and equal citizens, and not as dominated or manipulated or under pressure caused by an inferior political or social position' (1999: 14). Finally, Rawls's account of the scope of human rights falls short of the current formulation exemplified by the International Bill of Rights, comprising the UDHR, the ICCPR and the ICESCR. For Rawls, the purpose of human rights within a globally just order is as follows: 'they restrict the justifying reasons for war and its conduct, and they specify limits to a regime's internal autonomy (1999: 79). Gaining a sufficiently detailed understanding of Rawls's proposals in this regard requires an analysis of each of these elements.

Rawls's analysis of liberalism and his distinction between political and comprehensive liberalism have their origins in his *Political Liberalism*. Simplifying a complex account and series of arguments, Rawls argues that modern complex societies do not yield a reasonable consensus in support of comprehensive liberalism as a distinct account of the morally good life.[2]

---

[2]   See Kukathas and Pettit (1990) for a detailed analysis of Rawls's distinction between comprehensive and political liberalism.

Because not all who are subject to the jurisdiction of the 'liberal' state share
the values and ideals of comprehensive liberalism, and because this state of
affairs is 'reasonable', the moral legitimacy of the liberal state must be secured
upon a somewhat more procedural and less substantive basis. In effect, this
requires that the state refrain from discriminating against those individuals and
communities who, for example, do not consider personal autonomy to be the
principal ingredient for leading a good life. Similarly, it will require the liberal
state to refrain from prioritising forms of education which emphasise a primarily secular or religious world-view. Comprehensive liberalism is characterised
as no longer enjoying (if it ever did) a justified and reasonably privileged place
in determining the basis and scope of political authority. Political liberalism,
in contrast, seeks to secure conditions of mutually reciprocal respect amongst
diverse communities and individuals who adhere to potentially incommensurate comprehensive moral doctrines. Achieving this will require the state
adopting a certain distance from any substantive moral doctrine, including
comprehensive liberalism. The philosophical basis for Rawls's argument lies
in ethical pluralism.[3] Pluralism holds, in effect, that there are many different
ways to lead a morally good life. Some of these ways may even be incommensurate with one another. Thus, pluralism rejects the claim that moral value
can be evaluated or measured by reference to a single scale (such as utility) or
a single, purportedly ultimately valuable ideal (such as personal autonomy).
Rawls's commitment to and formulation of ethical pluralism extend beyond
the more conventional liberal understanding which seeks to restrict moral
legitimacy to those ideals and practices which comply with the central liberal
ideals of equality and individual liberty.

It would, I believe, be a mistake to view this development in Rawls's
thought as an abandonment of Kant in favour of Hobbes. Rawls was clearly
concerned to forestall the potential of the state to induce strife and conflict
through its too close association with one constituency amongst the many who
are subject to its jurisdiction. However, he did not thereby commit himself to
the principle that whatever prevents strife and conflict is necessarily, on these
grounds alone, to be welcomed. The pragmatist turn in his thought is tempered
by his continuing commitment to the principle of reciprocity which is fundamental to his earlier account of domestic justice. Rawls's concern to establish
a just global order upon the principle of reciprocity can be understood, if only
implicitly, as an attempt to avoid the charges levelled at those human rights
proselytisers accused of, inadvertently perhaps, seeking to impose the partial
values of the globally powerful upon the globally weak. It also, more explic-

---

[3]   For discussions of pluralism and its relevance for international ethics see Paul,
Miller and Paul, eds. 1994; Walzer, 1994.

itly, accords the kind of 'voice' to non-western peoples which an overly ethno-centric approach to human rights has been accused of suppressing. In according such prominence to the ideal of reciprocity, Rawls effectively seeks dramatically to broaden the constituency of legitimate participants in the debate concerning what the basis of a just global order ought to be. The terms of this debate are also thereby altered so that it is no longer to be understood as a process of 'us' enlightening 'them' in our values and ideals but rather, as with Mutua's proposal, opening up the terms of the debate in a manner which no longer privileges the discourse of one constituency over all others.

Adopting a less substantively prescriptive approach to the basis and scope of a globally just order does not entail an abandonment of human rights. However, in Rawls's view, it does require a certain paring down of the doctrine. Rawls argues that a just global order cannot simply extend respect to all extant cultures and societies. However, he also insists that such an order may comprise societies other than simply liberal ones. He addresses his account to what he refers to as liberal peoples and decent hierarchical societies. While liberal societies are characterised by their espousal of a comprehensive panoply of human rights, decent hierarchical societies are based upon a commitment to a more limited range of rights. Thus, the global order may require that such societies share a commitment to life, liberty, property and to formal equality, which Rawls describes as the core of human rights. However, they do not necessarily need thereby to commit to the more comprehensive range of human rights enshrined within most liberal constitutions. Also, and arguably most importantly, whilst political power must not be the sole preserve of a single constituency, decent hierarchical societies need not be committed to the principle of universal suffrage. Nor need it be necessary for every member of such societies to possess substantively equal opportunities to access and influence the principal decision-making fora. Finally, decent hierarchical societies are characterised as such by the absence of any necessary commitment to individualism (in its various forms) as essential for their normative legitimacy. The fundamental political unit is thereby more likely to be an association or community, rather than the individual citizen. Rawls insists that the comprehensive doctrines of such societies cannot be fully unreasonable. He writes, 'these doctrines must admit a sufficient measure of liberty of conscience and freedom of religion and thought, even if these freedoms are not extensive nor as equal for all members of the decent society as they are in liberal societies' (Rawls, 1999: 74).

For Rawls the law of peoples applies to both liberal and non-liberal societies alike. While war-like societies are excluded, he argues that casting membership in these terms serves to overcome the cultural partiality and limitations of an account of human rights as necessarily requiring a conversion to comprehensive liberal values and ideals. He clearly states that 'it is crucial that the Law of Peoples does not require decent societies to abandon or modify their religious institutions and adopt liberal ones' (Rawls, 1999: 121). For him, a globally just order does require the establishment and protection of a limited range of human rights as fundamental freedoms, but this does not amount to an insistence that the entire globe comply with 'western' civilisation. For Rawls, the Law of Peoples asks people to adopt a standpoint of 'fair equality with all other societies' (Rawls, 1999: 122). A commitment to this particular principle, he insists, is not a commitment to an exclusively western idea, since the concept of fair equality is not the sole preserve of western civilisation.

In their different ways, both Mutua and Rawls offer proposals for avoiding the ethnocentric partiality of an account of human rights as the globalisation of distinctly western values and ideals. Mutua aims to expand the sources for determining the basis and scope of human rights, while Rawls proposes the establishment of a hard core of fundamental human rights as the basis for securing a just global order. To this extent, their work represents two poles of a spectrum which seeks to achieve a greater degree of global impartiality for human rights. Their contributions to the debate surrounding universalism and relativism are significant to the extent that both offer alternative accounts of human rights to that which seeks to tie the doctrine's legitimacy and diffusion to an allegedly global process of modernisation, which, to some, appears veritably hegemonic and potentially suppressive of existing societal cultures. Thus, whereas Donnelly, for example, envisages human rights as a counterpart to a necessarily globalising process of structural transformation, writers such as Mutua, in particular, view this process in somewhat more jaundiced terms and as a process to be confronted and forestalled where it proves to be harmful. If human rights are to provide for this oppositional project, they must have a basis beyond the structural context of that which they provide a challenge to. Two examples of this are particularly pertinent: the collective rights of indigenous peoples and the relationship between human rights and Islam.

Indigenous peoples generally present particular difficulties for an overtly individualist approach to human rights. Their plight in the face of modernisation also provides a very telling example of how the extension of purportedly liberal constitutional rights has had little positive effect upon the lives of those for whom such traditions are largely alien. As Samson (2003) and Short (2008) have both demonstrated, the effects of the modernising colonialisation of the indigenous peoples of Canada and Australia have been generally catastrophic for those peoples. Previously long-established ways of life have been eroded and, in some cases, actively suppressed in the aim of assimilating these peoples within the modern state. An individualist approach to land title has served fundamentally to undermine whole communities' access to traditional lands, and traditional forms of economic subsistence have been targeted as economically unproductive and anachronistic. The morbidity and mortality statistics for both groups of indigenous peoples are appalling in such otherwise 'modern' and developed nation-states. Many indigenous peoples' representatives have pursued their political campaigns through appeals to collective rights claims, which, though they have achieved some limited success in respect of legal recognition, remain utterly incompatible with the predominantly individualist approach to rights claims that prevails in both jurisdictions. Some other indigenous peoples' representatives have gone even further and have requested that they merely be left alone, given the effects upon them of having fallen under the 'gaze' of a modern state. It is clear that the plight of indigenous peoples counters the advocacy of human rights as a mere counterpart to modernisation insofar as the remedies on offer have proven largely inadequate to the scale of the damage or incompatible with the world-views of those who wish to be protected from the modernisation process in the first place. An understanding of human rights as a counterpart and response to modernisation entails a corresponding conception of what constitutes a 'harm' which does not adequately translate into the world-views of indigenous peoples. In this case, the ethnocentricity of an account of human rights which defines both the ailment and the remedy in overly partial terms is clearly apparent. To this extent, one may tentatively suggest that the less ethnocentrically charged approach to human rights proposed by Mutua and Rawls would offer more scope for indigenous peoples' participation in a process for determining the appropriate basis and scope of human rights. One would expect, for example, such communities to accord very much more significance to collective rights claims than is typically the case within the more overtly individualist societal cultures of the world. One might also expect indigenous peoples' conceptions of autonomy to be very much more collectivist in character than the predominantly liberal conception of autonomy. A degree of suspicion surrounds such claims within conventional academic human rights discourse (Kukathas, 2003). An approach to human rights which did not presume that 'our' standards were necessarily correct for all would lend this discourse a greater degree of intellectual sophistication and provide a more effective forum in which the voices of suffering human beings might be better heard.

A rather more complex relationship concerns that between human rights and Islam. There are those, most notably Samuel Huntington (1996), who argue that Islam cannot adequately comply with the tenets of human rights. Similar sentiments have also been all too frequently expressed by self-declared representatives of 'Islam' in the context of complex geo-political circumstances and events and a desire to associate human rights as somehow 'belonging' to the West. In this context the charge of ethnocentricity is levelled in an apparent attempt by some to forestall the ambition of human rights and to pursue and secure an alternatively hegemonic power. Despite a common perception to the contrary, this constituency does not represent *the* Islamic perception and understanding of human rights. Indeed, as I argued earlier, cultural essentialism begins with a conception of geo-political and regional entities as reducing to a single, homogeneous entity. As there is no single 'West', so there is no single 'Islam'; significant variation of doctrinal inter- pretation and religious practice is well-documented. This has provided the basis for some Muslim human rights scholars to argue for the potential for developing an approach to human rights which is compatible with the spirit of human rights and with the tenets of Islam. The focus of this work has been a reinterpretation of Shari'a and is epitomised by the likes of Abdullah An'Naim (1991) and Fatima Mernissi (1991). In their respective ways, both authors have attempted to develop a significantly revised understanding of the ethical sources of Shari'a. In effect, they both attempt to liberate Shari'a from what they view as completely outdated and anachronistic tenets. Their project is thus premised on the claim that Islam is not necessarily and inherently opposed to religious freedom or gender equality, as is frequently claimed by opponents and supporters alike. It is perceived only as such as a consequence of a particularly conservative constituency of clerics gaining control of Islam in many parts of the world. This conservative constituency is not so much interested in promoting Islamic truths as in consolidating and extending their own political power. This is obviously greatly assisted by a general Islamic rejection of the liberal separation of the powers of state and religion. Islam is not restricted to the private sphere alone, but is viewed by its adherents as a code for all areas of life. Both authors recognise the extent of the obstacles to developing an account of human rights which may legitimately influence and contribute to the development of an ecumenical understanding of the basis and scope of human rights. However, against the likes of Huntington, they insist that this is possible and that the project would not merely entail complying with a 'western' conception of human rights but would contribute to an under- standing of human rights which Muslims need not consider to be entirely alien to their beliefs and practices.

In their different ways, the ecumenical approach and Rawls's account of human rights within a proposed law of peoples represent an acknowledgment of the perception some have of human rights as unduly indebted to a partial cultural outlook. They also offer the basis of a reformulated account of human rights which is genuinely more universal in its appreciation of the complexity of human communities. They both point to the pressing need to develop an account of human rights which does not require the assimilation of the 'other' within a predominantly individualist and secular discourse. A genuinely universal and sufficiently comprehensive account of human rights would necessitate the abolition of any such distinctions. This task has yet to be fully undertaken and engaged with. In developing this line of human rights theoris- ing, we must also note some potential pitfalls to and weaknesses in the general approach represented by the ecumenical approach and Rawls's Law of Peoples. These concerns centre upon the capacity of culture and religion to suppress and oppress their own members.

I have argued for the need to establish human rights upon a principal concern to alleviate and overcome systematic and significant human suffering. How we ultimately define what constitutes suffering is a deeply complex issue. A non-relativist acknowledgement of the importance of societal culture for human identity adds additional complexity to the issue. What constitutes material deprivation, for example, is to some extent a culturally relative phenomenon (Sen, 1999a). However, these kinds of questions resonate with theorists and academics but typically have less merit and value for those who continue to suffer systematically from political and economic oppression. For these people, being faced with the systematic threat of personal annihilation or political servitude typically suffices as confirmation of the objectivity of their plight. I have also argued that an aversion to or suspicion of human rights amongst some 'non-western' peoples must be seen in the light of the destruction which western powers have wrought throughout many parts of the world: for many, the West does not fit the bill of the typical 'saviour'. In recognising the basis for this suspicion it is also important, of course, to appeal to human rights as a mechanism for preventing, rather than legitimising, the abuse of power irrespective of who the abusers may happen to be. A genuinely universal and independent doctrine of human rights must eschew identification with or assimilation by any and all dominant or hegemonic powers.[4] A genuine account of human rights must seek, therefore, to prevent systematic and significant human suffering wherever it occurs. In this respect, both the ecumenical approach and Rawls's Law of Peoples fall short of what is required.

A concern for the importance of culture in influencing people's lives, wellbeing and identity has been widely recognised in recent decades (Kymlicka, 1989; Nussbaum, 2002; Sandel, 1982). Culture is now an integral part of contemporary political philosophy. The acknowledgement of culture's significance for understanding politics and morality has served to add greater sophistication and subtlety to contemporary analyses of how human beings may live relatively harmoniously together in an increasingly complex and interdependent world. Indeed, its importance has even extended to considerations of how liberal jurisdictions may require significant reformulations in order adequately to respect cultural differences, as we have seen in the work of John Rawls but as is also apparent in the work of Bhiku Parekh (2000) and Ayelet Shachar (2001). All of this work is similarly motivated by a desire to overcome the ethnocentric prejudices of aspects of liberal political philosophy.

---

[4]   I return to this point in the following chapter.

However, in pursuing this path from a human rights perspective, it is vitally important that we do not lose sight of the potential of societal culture to induce systematic suffering and oppression.

It is important to distinguish between two principles: a concern for protecting human rights as a means for overcoming systematic and significant human suffering and a commitment to the promotion of cultural autonomy. Some writers have failed clearly to distinguish between the two. Thus, Mutua supports a principle of the moral equivalency of cultures when he writes that 'proper human rights ought to assume that all cultures are equal' (2002: 109). In effect, Mutua extends the application of the equality principle from individuals to cultures. While this may seem ostensibly appropriate as a counterpart to an ethnocentric disposition towards other cultures, it goes too far in the assumption that a commitment to human rights can be reconciled with what amounts to an uncritical endorsement of all cultural practices and traditions. For a human rights theorist who values the principle of the equal moral value of all individuals Mutua's proposal will appear thoroughly unacceptable. Thus, the lack of formal equality experienced by women under Shari'a law has been frequently criticised as a violation of women's rights (McGoldrick, 2006; Othman, 1999; Saliyeh, 2003). Similar claims have also been made in respect of the social status of women within Hinduism. A commitment to individual equality lies deep within the core of the human rights doctrine and provides the principal obstacle to extending human rights claims to collective entities whilst simultaneously opposing the kind of proposal made by Mutua. While inequality can be a fundamental element of systematic human suffering and the denial of each human being's capacity to lead a minimally good life, I do not consider the principle to be sufficient for establishing the legitimacy of human rights, nor sufficient as a criterion for evaluating the relationship between human rights and societal cultures. However, when one shifts the focus towards systematic human suffering more generally one must still conclude that a commitment to human rights will not always allow for the moral validation of any and all cultural practices and beliefs. I have written elsewhere (Fagan, 2006) of the need to retain a critical perspective upon the potential of all societal cultures to induce systematic human suffering (see also Moller Okin, 1999). One must not simply assume either that all cultures are necessarily benign for all of their members or that those that are not will simply fade away as their dissonant members exercise the option to exit the community. Acknowledging the ontological properties and influences of societal culture entails recognising the extent to which cultural conditioning may serve to legitimise demonstrable suffering and oppression. Few, if any, cultures are completely homogeneous and self-enclosed. However an increasing focus upon so-called identity politics demonstrates the extent to which individuals' options for leading minimally good lives may be restricted by their membership of a given cultural community. A commitment to human rights requires a duty to offer effective protection against all forms of systematic and significant human suffering. The fact that the cause of any such suffering may have achieved a certain degree of cultural legitimacy should present no obstacle to a commitment to human rights. In practice, of course, this commitment runs the very real risk of simply reproducing the proselytising saviour mentality of some human rights advocates which this chapter has sought to criticise. Paternalism is, I believe, an integral feature of the human rights doctrine. What is essential, however, is how human rights are to be understood and to what extent this understanding suffers from unduly ethnocentric and partial cultural biases. Truly overcoming ethnocentricity will prove a very daunting challenge in the years to come.

CONCLUSION

This chapter has sought to analyse a particular myth of human rights which holds that the task of universalising the doctrine requires the exporting of western values and ideals to the rest of the world. I have argued that effectively promoting the legitimacy of human rights requires a greater critical appreciation of the potentially partial and ethnocentric elements of some parts of the theory and practice of human rights. Generally, I am advocating a greater degree of critical self-reflection within the human rights community. The timing seems opportune. I believe it is fair to characterise human rights as having entered a slightly more doubtful and reflexive stage in their historical development. A number of factors are likely to be significant in this regard: the end of the Cold War, the emergence of a distinctly post-colonial discourse in academic circles, the re-emergence of religious doctrine for many communities of the world, the failure of the wealthy countries to eradicate absolute poverty, the inability of the UN to prevent a number of recent and ongoing genocides and atrocities, the loss of moral authority incurred by the United States and its allies in the debacle that is Iraq. All of these have influenced the general perception of the moral authority of human rights. Human rights is a universal doctrine and it must achieve genuine universal authority if it is to realise even the modest aim of eradicating systematic and significant human suffering, quite apart from all of the other aspirations typically associated with the doctrine. The quest for this degree of moral authority is, perhaps, more daunting today than ever before in the modern history of the doctrine. The need to do so remains as pressing and urgent as ever. This chapter has argued that an acknowledgment of ethnocentricity is crucial in this regard. So too is an acknowledgement that the West is not typically viewed as the moral saviour by those who have suffered human rights abuses at its hands. What is required is greater dialogue and understanding amongst those who recognise the imperative of overcoming human suffering. However, in pursuing this path, we must not lose sight of an essential attribute of human rights, which consists of the doctrine's critical independence from the exercise of mere power and privilege. Overcoming ethnocentricity and cultural essentialism requires a refusal to allow human rights to become the sole preserve of any societal culture.

4. Globalisation, human rights and the modern nation-state

INTRODUCTION

Chapter 4 shifts the focus of discussion from the more overtly theoretical to the more recognisably institutional domain of human rights. The principal purpose of this chapter is to engage critically with a particular misunderstanding of the geo-political realities of contemporary human rights practice. The specific misunderstanding I address in this chapter concerns a view of the modern nation-state as the principal obstacle to realising human rights' globalising ambition. This misunderstanding is, I believe, most apparent among human rights enthusiasts and advocates who most likely associate with civil society or non-governmental organisations whose principal adversary is the state and who, not surprisingly, come to view the state as the main obstacle to successfully realising their human rights goals. I assess the role of the modern nation-state in the protection and promotion of human rights principles. I consider both normative and empirical assessments and representations of the state, including those typically presented by advocates of cosmopolitanism and realism. I argue that human rights are often closely associated with a cosmopolitan ethical outlook which is itself considered to be a benign counterpart to globalisation. While this is obviously consistent with the universalising ambition of human rights, I argue that one consequence of this association is a diminution of the state's importance in upholding human rights. Typically, human rights advocates view the state as the principal violator of human rights and turn to ostensibly cosmopolitan principles and institutions for a potential alternative to a geo-politics founded upon sovereign states' violation of international human rights standards. I argue that while it is normatively correct to establish a commitment to human rights upon cosmopolitan principles, representing the state in primarily negative terms misrepresents the continuing power of the sovereign state and perpetuates an overly one-dimensional view of the state which obscures the state's capacity to protect human rights. To misunderstand the state as primarily a violator of human rights is ultimately unhelpful to the human rights cause. This chapter argues for the need to recognise the realities of global politics and the limitations of those institutions typically viewed as transcending the constraints of state sovereignty in the aim of encouraging a more constructive and proactive engagement with states' role in upholding a global system which proclaims the value of human rights but has still actively to practise this proclaimed commitment. As the world is presently structured, human rights cannot be achieved without utilising state power and resources.

COSMOPOLITANISM AND HUMAN RIGHTS

There are two clearly apparent grounds for the misunderstanding this chapter seeks to address. First, the empirical fact that the principal violators of human rights remain individual nation-states and, second, the often only latent influence of ethical cosmopolitanism upon many people's commitment to and understanding of human rights. The first ground is, unfortunately, self-explanatory. Only a complete fool would seek to argue that some other single institution or phenomenon is more culpable than the state in the continuing violation of human rights in the world today. The second ground, as my allusion to its latent influence suggests, requires a rather more detailed explanation. What is ethical cosmopolitanism and how does it affect the misunderstanding this chapter is concerned with?

It has already been established that human rights are founded upon universalising moral principles. Many view human rights as a manifestation of globalisation and as offering opportunities to curb abuse of power. In the previous chapter, I argued for the need to re-address these claims in the light of criticisms that some people's understanding of human rights has fallen short of genuine universalism and has espoused, instead, overly partial values and ideals: all too often, human rights universalism has been associated with a set of globalising 'western' phenomena and has failed adequately to engage with other cultural frameworks. Against this, cosmopolitanism is an ethical doctrine which seeks to identify legitimate principles for regulating global institutions and relationships in a manner that is consistent with a commitment to human rights. The need for specifying this particular approach as 'cosmopolitan' grows out of a recognition that not all universalising doctrines can be described as wholly or sufficiently supportive of human rights. Utilitarianism is a universalising moral doctrine. However, its fundamental emphasis upon aggregative measures of moral value is typically viewed as thoroughly incompatible with human rights' focus upon the inalienable rights of the sovereign individual (Dworkin, 1990). Christianity and Islam are similarly universalising doctrines. However, the very essence of their religiosity will have little or no appeal to all of those who commit to secular or agnostic values and ideals. Simply being a universalising doctrine is clearly not sufficient to establish a doctrine's compatibility with the spirit of human rights. Thus, numerous writers and practitioners have referred to human rights as based upon a specifically cosmopolitan ethical outlook and commitments. These include academics such as Sharon Anderson-Gold (2001), Brian Barry (1991), Simon Caney (2005) and Thomas Pogge (1992). A commitment to cosmopolitanism would also extend beyond academia to include most, if not all, former secretaries-general of the United Nations and iconic political leaders such as Nelson Mandela. So, what specifically is cosmopolitanism?

Cosmopolitanism is a moral and political position which shares with universalism the claim that there exist universally valid moral principles for governing relations between all relevant political agents. Thomas Pogge (1992) has argued that cosmopolitanism possesses three constitutive elements: individualism, universalism and generality. Individualism, as has been discussed previously, is based upon the claim that the ultimate moral unit is the sovereign individual. The principal philosophical origins of this view are viewed by Anderson-Gold (2001) as lying in the moral philosophy of Immanuel Kant. Within the contemporary doctrine of cosmopolitanism a commitment to individualism does not, necessarily, entail the view that collective constituencies have no moral value but that the ultimate arbiter of moral value consists of the sovereign individual. Cosmopolitans are, therefore, typically not supportive of collective rights claims *per se* (Barry, 2001). Universalism refers specifically to the attribution of equal moral value to all individuals everywhere. While distinct differences in the possession of material or symbolic capital have determinative effects upon individuals' actual lives, cosmopolitans argue that these differences should have no bearing upon individuals' moral standing. They will also typically go further and argue that the distribution of material and symbolic capital should be evaluated in the light of the criterion of moral equality (see Pogge, 1992). Finally, generality expresses the globalising character of a cosmopolitan ethical outlook. Thus, a concern for the equal moral status of all individuals must apply to all human beings everywhere and is not restricted to, or contingent upon, more overtly local associations or communities. On this view, moral relationships transcend social, political, economic and geographic boundaries to encompass a single, global moral community. Morally speaking then, human rights obligations do not begin and end at national borders, but extend to encompass all peoples everywhere. Simon Caney summarises this final element when he writes that 'all persons are of equal moral worth and everyone has duties to other human beings' (2005: 5).

Cosmopolitanism orients and directs our moral and political focus and concern away from the solely local and partial and towards the truly global. From this perspective we are all citizens of the world. Cosmopolitans, such as Caney, argue that the global political realm should be governed in accordance with the three central elements of cosmopolitanism: universalism, individualism and generality. From this perspective, all human beings are of equal moral standing within a single political space. This single space is itself viewed as being increasingly established through the process of globalisation, through which previously relatively discrete communities are increasingly assimilated within a single material and interdependent framework. Suffice it to say, for the moment, that human rights is a recognisably cosmopolitan doctrine and is considered by many as a benign manifestation of material globalisation. In its theoretical guise, if not yet entirely and always in its practical guise, the human rights doctrine holds that all human beings are of equal moral standing and are entitled to adequate forms of protection and treatment, irrespective of where they happen to have been born. The global political realm is increasingly a very real and tangible place and should, on this view, be regulated in accordance with fundamental human rights principles.

The cosmopolitan vision of a global political order founded upon respect for human rights has profound implications for questions of institutional design. It is not sufficient simply to repeat a cosmopolitan mantra. What is required is the establishment of institutions capable of pursuing and achieving the doctrine's aspiration of equal human rights for all, regardless of where each human being happens to live. Typically, cosmopolitans view the sovereign nation-state as constituting a general obstacle to realising the aim of human rights equality. Thomas Pogge (1992) is an example in this regard. Pogge bases his vision of a reformed global order upon an appeal to a cosmopolitan political morality, founded upon a commitment to the equal moral value of all individual human beings. He views the current global order as fundamentally at odds with this aspiration. For Pogge, the principal element in need of reform is the legal and political function of national sovereignty. Put simply, Pogge views national sovereignty as normatively at odds with the ambition of human rights, and as providing a practical mechanism by which individual nation-states can themselves actively abuse human rights or refrain from any interventional action in preventing other sovereign states from abusing human rights. Pogge argues that the global political sphere requires a radical reform if human rights principles are to be fully protected. More specifically he proposes the empowerment of institutions and agents both above and below the level of the current nation-state as providing the basis by which national sovereignty may be eroded and curtailed in the name of more adequately realising the ambition of human rights and towards the establishment of a genuinely cosmopolitan global political order.

Pogge's proposals clearly imply that the current global order is not generally aligned with a sufficiently established commitment to human rights. This runs counter to the general claims espoused by the likes of Jack Donnelly (2002) and Louis Henkin (1990), who both characterise the global political sphere as largely consistent with and expressive of the spirit of human rights.

Donnelly, in particular, has explicitly argued that increasing globalisation has been accompanied by the rise of human rights as a veritably global hegemonic force, in the light of which most (if not all) nation-states seek to regulate their behaviour with other states and with their own citizens. Pogge's claims might also cause some puzzlement amongst those who consider the United Nations (UN) as providing the kind of framework he envisages but claims the world currently lacks. For many, the UN in respect of its design and intent, if not always in respect of its actions, provides the definitive cosmopolitan political institution required for upholding a global commitment to equal human rights for all individual human beings. The importance of the UN in this respect entails a closer examination in the light of this chapter's particular focus.

To many, the UN appears as the quintessential cosmopolitan institution and typically represents the principal inter-governmental organisation involved in the protection and promotion of human rights. The role and importance of the UN in establishing international human rights law are undeniable. In this respect, the UN is the institutional fount of many of the principal human rights treaties and covenants. These treaties and covenants have produced a regulatory regime which covers a vast range of human activities. The UN also comprises bodies and agents whose task is to scrutinise the implementation of international human rights law. These comprise, for example, the recently reformed human rights committee, and the various specialist agencies, such as UNHCR, UNIFEM, UNESCO and the like. One may also cite the various special *rapporteurs* as fundamental to the UN's human rights work. While the specialist agencies typically occupy a high public profile and exposure in their attempts to secure people's human rights, the human rights committee and the work of the special *rapporteurs* operate within the institutional body of the UN. The work of special rapporteurs and human rights committees has frequently served to identify and expose the systematic failure of member states to implement the human rights instruments which they have ratified. Many general comments and specific country reports have been damning and unequivocal in their condemnation of human rights abuses. In a slightly more subjective vein, many have commented on the extent to which the spirit of human rights permeates many corners of the UN's work. On first impressions, the UN's cosmopolitan credentials appear unimpeachable. However, first impressions can be deceptive, and this is particularly so in this regard.

Despite the unquestionable commitment to human rights of many of those associated with the organisation, the UN itself is best described as a contradictory organisation, one whose public face is not fully supported by its institutional design and organisation. It is an inter-governmental organisation with clear universalising aspirations. However, its ability practically to protect and promote human rights is restricted by the simple fact that it is comprised of individual nation-states whose own self-interests may come into conflict with the pursuit of universal human rights. The ability of states to prioritise self-interest over human rights is secured in various ways. Most importantly, the principle of national sovereignty is enshrined within the UN Charter, Article 2(7) of which explicitly proscribes against the UN 'intervening in matters which are essentially the domestic jurisdiction of any state'. There are some exceptions to this provision, most notably the case of genocide, but this notwithstanding, Article 2(7) has played a prominent role in frustrating the practical realisation of human rights principles. There are countless examples where the article has given legal protection to human-rights-violating member states and enabled them to continue abusing and denying the human rights of those they ought (in a cosmopolitan/human rights sense) to be protecting.

Member states are expected to ratify and implement the fundamental human rights covenants, but this is not universally achieved. The former Soviet Union refused to ratify the ICCPR and the United States has consistently refused to ratify the ICESCR. However, where a member state has ratified a covenant or treaty it is subject to the scrutinising mechanisms which aim to ensure that these legal promises are upheld. The UN abounds with such mechanisms. Thus, the special *rapporteur* for health conducts country studies and presents reports detailing the progress member states are making in realising their human rights obligations in this sphere (Hunt, 1996). Many of these reports are highly critical and identify numerous failings. However, in this respect, the UN has no ultimate power to ensure that member states adequately comply with their legal obligations. It can cajole and name and shame but it has no ultimate authority or capacity to enforce compliance. One might counter that ostensibly more serious human rights violations are liable to fall foul of the UN Security Council, which does have the capacity, under some circumstances, to enforce compliance through the deployment of sanctions and armed force if necessary. Unfortunately, the Security Council's record in this respect is patchy, at best. All too often, effective action has been prevented by the power of the veto vote cast by any one of the five permanent members. In these instances, partial national interests prevail over the demands of a commitment to protect human rights. While some may be inclined to single out China in this instance, each of the other permanent members has also exercised its veto in recent years in ways which have adversely affected the human rights of countless numbers of people.

It is important to be clear on the extent of the UN's ability to protect and promote human rights. Many aspects of the UN's work undeniably have promoted and continue to promote human rights: the human rights of people across the world would most likely be far more threatened if the UN did not exist. However, the institutional structure of the UN defies its cosmopolitan ethos insofar as the principle of national sovereignty enjoys centre-stage. Put simply, human rights are more likely to be protected where doing so coincides with the self-interests particularly of the more powerful member states: human rights have become, to some extent, a tool in the pursuit of national self-interest. Where protecting human rights runs counter to the perceived self-interests of member states then, unfortunately, the UN has little practical capacity for prioritising the demands of human rights. Michael Freeman's description of the UN exemplifies its limitations: '[t]he UN is a club of states, represented by governmental leaders, and, notwithstanding their conflicts of interest and ideology, they have a common interest in mutual accommodation. This may inhibit robust action for human rights where such action might upset the diplomatic apple-cart' (2002: 53–54).

A sufficiently clear-headed assessment of the UN in its current structure and organisation entails drawing some rather sombre conclusions. While the UN represents for many the benign face of globalisation and the predominant cosmopolitan mechanism for realising equal human rights for all, its actual structure and organisation point us in a different direction, wherein the power of the nation-state appears largely undiminished by globalising forces and international human rights campaigns. This particular direction is best signposted with the label of Realism.

REALISM, NATIONAL SOVEREIGNTY AND HUMAN RIGHTS

I have argued that human rights must be understood, broadly speaking, as a cosmopolitan doctrine. What accompanies this association is a relative disregard for or hostility towards the nation-state. On this view, the nation-state is either the principal violator of human rights (which is true) or simply increasingly irrelevant to upholding human rights claims, given the spread of globalising forces and constituencies. Those who hold to this view will often simply assume that the UN provides the definitive confirmation of the institutional establishment of cosmopolitan human rights principles that transcend national frontiers and appeals to national sovereignty. I have presented these views as comprising a damaging misunderstanding of the continuing power and influence of the nation-state as exemplified by the structure and organisation of the UN: the very organisation that many point to in support of their cosmopolitan beliefs actually demonstrates the opposite. The nation-state remains the fundamental unit for global politics. This requires a sufficiently detailed and sophisticated analysis of the nation-state and its effects upon and implications for establishing an effectively global human rights regime. To this end, one must turn to international relations and realism.

A deeper theme of this particular work consists of my attempt to caution against the view that human rights have come to exercise a profound influence upon human relations. A supporter of human rights has good reasons to avoid such complacency. Despite claims to the contrary, many areas of the globe do not fully support human rights, even in the relatively modest form which I advocate. As I argued in the previous chapter, some have simply assumed that this opposition is largely restricted to 'non-western' communities who have not, it is assumed, been sufficiently schooled in the moral authority of 'our' values and ideals. This assumption grossly distorts non-western communities. It also, however, thoroughly misrepresents 'western' commitments to human rights. Many western scholars and policy-makers have been and remain sceptical as to the basis for or the efficacy of human rights in a complex world. This scepticism extends well beyond the academic realm, but a discussion of one academic approach to understanding global political relations provides an excellent example of what is at stake and what is in dispute.

Realism presents a radically differing view of global politics from that one typically finds amongst supporters of cosmopolitanism. Realism, and its later variant neo-realism, includes the likes of Hans Morganthau (1951), George Keenan (1964) and Kenneth Waltz (1979). Beyond academia it would be fair to say that realism is the dominant model espoused by principal political agents and actors. Understanding the differences between an ethical cosmopolitan outlook and realism requires drawing a distinction between empirical and normative criteria. Thus, realism is based upon two central claims: an empirical claim that states' actions and policies are principally or entirely determined by considerations of national self-interest and a normative claim that pursuing national self-interest is precisely what states ought to do. Realism is fundamentally state-centric. It differs from cosmopolitanism in respect of its focus upon the single state. It also claims to differ from cosmopolitanism in respect of its normative espousal of national self-interest. Thus, a cosmopolitan might accept that states do all too often act in pursuit of what they consider to be their self-interest, but that this is not a normatively desirable principle, given its likely implications for the protection of human rights. Against this, realists have generally argued that cosmopolitanism exaggerates the influence and importance of international institutions and organisations. They also argue that the single most important principle which does and should govern the global political realm is that of nation-state sovereignty. Individual nation-states must not be compelled by other states or international bodies and agencies to agree to anything which runs against their particular interests. Nation-states differ across the globe, and so do each nation-state's interests. This fact excludes the legitimacy of compelling all nation-states to adhere to a single moral and political code. This principle ultimately dates back to the 1648 Treaty of Westphalia and has achieved a veritably totemic status within international relations circles. It is also, of course, firmly established within the UN Charter. The principle of state sovereignty is also central to the international law of armed conflict and humanitarian intervention. With few exceptions, sovereign nation-states may be said to enjoy a significant degree of negative liberty *vis-à-vis* other sovereign states. The principle of state sovereignty is central to realism and is central to the structure and continuing organisation of global politics. What effects does this have for the protection and promotion of human rights?

The trend within human rights circles is towards a view of state sovereignty as somehow inconsistent with the demands of human rights. I have already alluded to a catalogue of instances where UN action in support of human rights commitments has been prevented or constrained by the exercise of state sovereignty. Realism offers an explanation and ostensive justification for this state of affairs. Put simply, the demands of a global commitment to human rights and the specific demands of national self-interest need not always cohere. Indeed, they often appear to be thoroughly incompatible. Where this is the case, the legal weight of state sovereignty will serve to trump a commitment to human rights. Accurately gauging the status of state sovereignty appears to contradict the status and efficacy of human rights. It also may appear to entail an acceptance of the validity of realism. On this view a commitment to human rights is ultimately conditional upon whether, in any given instance, this commitment can be shown to be in the national self-interests of those who are required to take action. At this point it is important to recognise that, for many realists at least, the dispute is not between morality as represented by human rights and the amorality of national self-interest. As Hans Morganthau (1951), in particular, has argued, the dispute between realists and cosmopolitans is not a dispute between amoralists and moralists but, rather, is better understood as a dispute between two rival moral perspectives. He insists that promoting national self-interest is the morally correct action to take. He argues that states have a fundamental moral duty towards their own citizens first and foremost. On this view, morally valid principles are those based upon recognition that the individual nation-state remains the principal and fundamental political entity in the globalised political realm, and that each individual nation-state must prioritise its own citizens' interests above those of any other state. We are not, and should not be, citizens of the world. One may disagree with the moral claims of realists, but one should avoid misrepresenting them.

While this adds real weight to my depiction of the alternative view as a basic misunderstanding of the current status of human rights in a global political setting, the support provided seems somewhat counter-productive to the ends of a commitment to human rights as a means for confronting systematic and significant human suffering. I may appear to have thrown the baby out with the bath-water. Can this conclusion be avoided? Articulating an answer to this question should begin with a critical assessment of realism as a distinctly academic model of political behaviour. One may pursue this through distinguishing between the empirical and normative aspects of realism. I shall consider each in turn.

One may assume that the empirical basis of realism's account of how global politics is conducted is very solid. On the face of it, realism certainly appears to offer a more accurate account of international political behaviour than its cosmopolitan counterpart. Accepting this claim does not, of course, entail the conclusion that this is morally desirable: one's moral criteria need not ultimately always reduce to empirical political realities. It does, however, apparently entail accepting the evidence of one's senses. Individual nation-states are constantly referring to national interests in explaining why they act in the way they do. Principal political agents and policy-makers seem to view what they do in realist terms. On this view, cosmopolitanism seems more at home in an academic's study than in the real world of competing nation-states. However, there are good reasons to hesitate before concluding that realism is, if not morally desirable, at least empirically verifiable. Thus, realism cannot and does not accurately describe all that occurs in the global political realm. It is a fact that individual nation-states have agreed to limit some (albeit limited) degree of their own sovereignty through membership of international and regional bodies such as the UN, the European Union, the Organisation of African States, ASEAN and the like. This limitation of sovereignty is characteristically justified by appeal to national interests. Similarly, individual states differ very significantly in the degree to which they are prepared to forego some part of their own sovereignty. In this respect, compare Scandinavian states' policies on overseas aid with that of the United States. Thus, realism may account for a large part of how states act, but it does not tell the whole story: not all facts point to a realist conclusion. Some states and most international bodies are significantly influenced by more recognisably cosmopolitan concerns and seek to act in accordance with them.

Remaining with the empirical test, a serious and important question needs to be raised about the very concept of self-interest that lies at the heart of realism. Why should we accept that simply whatever a state does is motivated by self-interest? We must ask precisely who is in a position to determine what a single nation-state's interests are. This, in turn, raises questions of political legitimacy. To what extent are the representatives of any given nation-state legitimately authorised to act in this capacity? How have those empowered to act in the state's self-interest achieved this position? These questions concern both how self-interest is conceptualised and how some gain power to represent and determine what a nation-state's interests are presented as being. Thus, empirically speaking not all agents do always act in their own self-interest. Assuming that any agent (an individual or an entire nation-state) knows accurately what its interests actually are (a large assumption in itself), there are many instances of agents acting in ways contrary to their interests being momentarily overcome by some less considered impulse or motive. Factors such as the breadth and depth of knowledge are relevant in this respect. Was the agent fully and transparently cognisant of all relevant information when determining which interests should prevail? In a context as complex as global political affairs it seems somewhat optimistic to assume that this particular criterion is always satisfied. An example of the criterion of cognisance may be readily seen in the case of some western states' commitment to the so-called 'war on terror' since the terrible events of 11 September 2001. There is no doubt that this campaign has been conducted in the name of self-interest, but can it really be in the interests of even very powerful states to create so many new enemies in pursuit of their objectives? Is it not at the very least credible to claim that individual nation-states' interests might be better served by recognising and respecting more cosmopolitan ideals in the form of international laws and treaties which seek to uphold human rights principles, at home and abroad and without discrimination?

One might also add the potentially complicating issue of competing or conflicting interests within a single nation-state. In some instances it is perfectly conceivable that the economic interests of a nation-state may require actions which run counter to the political interests of the same state. An example of this can be found in nation-states whose economies include a significant arms-manufacturing industry exporting to countries which are unpopular with the electorate. National interests do not, necessarily, reduce to a single scale of measurement or criterion.

Finally, one must raise an empirical question concerning how power-holders have come to occupy their position. This question can take a normative form and, as such, will be considered at length in the following chapter. It can also, however, take an empirical form which focuses upon the claim that those who occupy power in a single nation-state are genuinely seeking to promote the interests of their own people. Who are the 'people' in this context? Many states comprise a number of diverse peoples. Empirically speaking there are many examples of individual nation-states which have openly acted against the interests of some parts of their citizenry. Those which have waged these campaigns have often done so in the name of national security or social harmony but, in actuality, these campaigns are more accurately understood as attempts by power-holders to extend their own more partial interests over those they have gained power over. In this respect, witness the continuing internal repression in countries such as Zimbabwe and Myanmar, to name but two from a depressingly long list.

From an empirical perspective, the phenomena cited above raise serious questions for those who assume that the world complies with the realist model of it. In the debate between cosmopolitanism and realism this is significant, given the current global geo-political order. One conclusion that may be drawn from the examples cited above is that, at the very least, the world is far more complex than realism would have us believe. However, this is not a positive argument in favour of cosmopolitanism. Nor does it add weight to the assumption that global politics is oriented towards human rights rather than more narrow national self-interest. Simply that realism has empirical issues does not justify concluding that cosmopolitanism fares any better. In this respect, it is probably fair to say that aspects of the global political realm do provide evidence for cosmopolitanism. The existence of international state bodies might be cited. Similarly, one could say that the increasing existence of international non-governmental organisations (INGOs) and numerous other global non-governmental networks points to the existence of political agents which do not share the state-centric account of realism. While these are significant, they do not serve wholly to falsify a view of the global political order as oriented more towards protecting national sovereignty than upholding human rights commitments. The empirical weaknesses of realism are, however, significant to developing an account of how the power of states may be steered towards protecting human rights, rather than paying lip service to them or openly violating them. I turn to this in the final section of this chapter. Before I attempt to present such an account, it is important to complete the critical analysis of realism through an analysis of its normative claims.

As I have discussed earlier in this book, resorting to morality and moral arguments to defend one's position can be fraught with potential problems. First and foremost is the problem of moral subjectivism; the view that morality is ultimately, like beauty, in the eye of the beholder. In this specific context, we can confidently expect human rights advocates to condemn realism as morally deficient, given the doctrine's evaluation of human rights: one would expect nothing less of the human rights community. The very fact of this moral condemnation does not, however, establish the validity of the claim. While some will continue to argue that the subjectivity of morality can never be overcome (see Williams, 1985), it is possible morally and critically to analyse a doctrine in the light of its own internal claims, rather than simply counter-pose one doctrine with another in order to find the one disapproved of to be morally deficient. If one adopts this standpoint with respect to realism's normative claims and assumptions, the doctrine is vulnerable to criticism. Three areas stand out as particularly important.

First and foremost realists cannot argue that simply because something is done in a particular way we are justified in concluding that it ought to be done in this way. Facts do not, of and by themselves, serve morally to justify themselves, so to speak. Romans fed Christians to the lions, much of the world throughout much of its history has treated women as inferior beings, millions of slaves were shipped from Africa to Europe and the Americas, and the Nazis sought to eradicate the Jews: all of these are facts; none of them should be viewed as anything other than morally reprehensible. Empirical facts do not offer independent moral justification for themselves. Nor does this mean that the validity of our moral claims is conditional upon their being widely accepted or politically validated. As I have argued earlier, part of the importance of human rights consists of the element of critical independence they enjoy from the material realities surrounding them. Human rights cannot be wholly detached from these realities, but nor must they simply reduce to them. The human rights community has a very real interest in retaining an awareness of this particular aspect of the doctrine if human rights are to avoid becoming merely tools for political manipulation.

Moving on to a second normative issue, realism is founded upon the normative claim that the pursuit of national self-interest is a good thing. Many accept this to be true, but why? Why should fellow citizens have greater moral claims upon one another than citizens across national borders? Many, if not all, national boundaries have a certain 'artificial' character to them after all, and are the product of a complex interplay of political and economic forces (Anderson, 1983). Few, if any, individual nation-states can be rightly considered as perfect embodiments of some pristine and primordial peoples. Indeed, most nation-states are more accurately perceived as polyethnic constituencies. This degree of internal diversity has raised serious issues of what, if anything, can be said to hold those communities together as single national units (Kymlicka, 1995). The very worst symptom of this phenomenon consists of the ethnic cleansing witnessed in parts of Africa and the Balkans. Ethnic and religious diversity raises serious issues for determining what a single nation's interests might be and even for what a single nation might consist of. Despite this, realism holds that, at least when facing one another, there is a moral difference between peoples on opposite sides of a single border. If this is the case, the relatively arbitrary and artificial nature of border construction provides an insecure foundation for such normative claims. I will consider the question of global moral relationships in detail in Chapter 6. Suffice it to say for the present that the realist's normative clam that the moral duties we owe to fellow members of the same national community must take precedence over the potential claims of 'outsiders' is undermined by the precariousness of the very construction of insiders and outsiders in a national context.

Finally, and remaining with the issue of national self-interest, we can also question the claim that individual nation-states are best placed to protect the interests of their citizens. This is a normative claim which lacks sufficiently robust empirical evidence. The global inequality of resources is characterised by a situation in which some states are incapable of adequately protecting and promoting the interests of their citizens. This systemic feature of the global political realm underlies claims by many that the people of such states are entitled to assistance and support from other nation-states and international

bodies. In this respect, in some cases the interests of citizens of some countries
may be better served precisely by the diminution of state sovereignty, given
their states' unwillingness or inability to provide the resources and protections
required. This extends beyond episodic humanitarian intervention to encompass the very basis and structure of the global distribution of resources, which
I consider in Chapter 6. For the moment, it serves to falsify the realist claim
that the single nation-state is necessarily best placed to provide for its own
without 'interference' or intervention from without.

The discussion of this section and its analysis of realism have brought us to
a veritable impasse or ostensibly frustrating juncture. I have sought to challenge the misunderstanding which over-emphasises the current power and
ability of human rights to regulate global politics. I have argued that, while a
commitment to human rights obviously remains morally valuable, we must
not overlook or ignore the global political framework within which national
sovereignty and the pursuit of what is perceived as national interest will often
frustrate and restrict the pursuit of human rights. This is not to say or imply
that human rights have no value or effect in the current global order. Clearly,
individual nation-states continue to commit to human rights principles and
some of them even attempt to go beyond paying mere lip service to them. The
UN also remains the single most important global institution for upholding the
cosmopolitan values upon which human rights are based. However, the over-
all success of the human rights project has been and continues to be significantly affected by the continuing power of states and a general tendency to
prioritise more partial interests and concerns where these appear to conflict
with the requirements of a satisfactory commitment to human rights. In
demonstrating and analysing the misunderstanding this chapter is concerned
with, I appear to have only testified to the current inadequacies and weaknesses of the doctrine. This is not, however, without merit. We must work from
where we are and in full knowledge and understanding of the context in which
we seek to enhance human rights' global efficacy. To this end, a hard-headed
appraisal of the obstacles which confront this aspiration is required and has
potential value. The value of these lessons learnt, however, depends upon how
they inform subsequent attempts to establish and defend human rights. The
following section concludes this chapter with an attempt to indicate areas in
which current realities may be accepted and revised in ways that enhance,
rather than diminish, human rights.

WORKING WITH THE STATE AND DEFENDING HUMAN RIGHTS

The argument and discussion presented in this chapter confront the human rights community with a rather difficult and uncomfortable reality. The nation-state remains the single worst violator of human rights. It does not, of course, have a monopoly of this particular title, but the power of the state provides the basis by which whole populations' fundamental rights may be systematically violated. The capacity of the state to violate human rights is effectively bolstered by the principle of national sovereignty. With a few exceptions such as genocide and torture, sovereign states retain the option of recognising or rejecting international human rights covenants. Most sovereign states of the globe have ratified a comprehensive array of human rights instruments. On an initial viewing this might appear to contradict the somewhat 'negative' vision I have been outlining. However, even after having states ratifying human rights instruments, the principle of national sovereignty provides a mechanism for preventing and obstructing external pressure to implement the provisions of these instruments: human rights are more often preached than practised. Given the state's reputation and track record in this regard, it is not surprising that many human rights advocates have come to abandon hope in transforming the state into an instrument for protecting, rather than abusing, human rights. The establishment of INGOs and an increasingly globalising civil society testify to the desire of many human rights advocates to by-pass the state altogether. Although entirely understandable, I fear that this tendency will generally serve to delay and further frustrate the realisation of human rights ambition.

Despite globalising economic, social and technological developments, the single nation-state remains the predominant political actor in the world today. Even relatively ineffective and impoverished states possess a degree of relative power which far exceeds that of any other powerful bodies or institutions. Powerful states continue to exert a profound influence upon global economic markets. They continue to wage war. They continue to regulate the flow of populations and migration. They retain the power of life over death. The realist model outlined above suggests the existence of a necessary conflict between the pursuit of national self-interest and the promotion of global human rights. For those national power-holders who have little manifest interest in the restriction of their power or the diminution of resources, this vision is obviously deeply attractive. However, I have argued that realism is vulnerable to a number of criticisms which impact upon both its empirical characterisation of the globe and its normative espousal of partial self-interest as the be-all-and-end-all of international politics. I have shown that states are prepared to delegate some part of their sovereignty through membership of regional and global inter-governmental institutions, albeit in ways designed to enhance rather than diminish their power and influence. I have also challenged the basis upon which groups of individuals come to occupy those positions from which national self-interest is determined. Finally, I have also challenged the presumption that a nation-state can be assumed to possess an ultimate set of generally agreed upon interests, given the internal diversity and complexity of most nation-states. Realism, I conclude, does not ultimately stack up and suffers from too many precarious premises and over-simplistic empirical claims to be worthy of our full acceptance. Where does this leave human rights?

The two illustrative extremes of human rights' relationship with the state can be seen in the consequences of a failed state, such as Somalia, or an all too effectively repressive state, such as North Korea. Between these extremes lie a range of developed and developing states which are more or less willing and capable of protecting human rights. All states violate human rights: some do so irregularly or infrequently; others do so as a matter of course. Despite this, I am arguing for the need for human rights supporters to engage constructively with nation-states in order better to secure the means for overcoming systematic and significant human suffering. This engagement with the state requires theoretical and practical guidance and action. In respect of theory, there is a pressing need to re-examine and critically analyse the concept of self-interest, since this is crucial to those justifications of state inaction or lack of concern for human rights. This is a complex task, which can be only briefly canvassed here. The process initially requires the raising of questions; such as, who determines what a nation's self-interests are? How have they come to occupy this position? What, if any, ends provide the criteria for identifying and according weight to a profile of national self-interests? The first two questions concern issues of political legitimacy and representation. These will be considered in greater detail in the next chapter. The third question, however, raises the issue of the potential status and importance of a comprehensive commitment to human rights as the potential linchpin of a global organisation of nation-states. The specific question which emerges from this concern is the following: is it not possible that individual nation-states' interests are better served within a political framework which is basically respectful of human rights as ends in themselves, rather than standing as merely expedient political tools for the pursuit of partial and apparent gain?

One theorist who has answered this question in the affirmative is Rein Mullerson (1997). Mullerson accepts the cosmopolitan basis of a commitment to human rights. However, he is critical of the conventional disregard for the state that accompanies some cosmopolitan theorising. Mullerson insists that the modern nation-state is a reality which cannot be ignored and must be constructively engaged with if human rights are to be better protected. Similarly, he views the most effective route to achieving this engagement to lie within the concept and ideal of self-interest as encompassed within the notion of national sovereignty. Contrary to other prevailing views, Mullerson argues that human rights may be defended as consistent with, rather than potentially antithetical to, the principle of national sovereignty. The basis of his argument is a rejection of the claim that national sovereignty is an end in itself and is valuable and legitimate only to the extent that it positively contributes to more ultimate ends and interests. He proceeds to argue that all nation-states have a basic and fundamental interest in global and domestic peace and stability. Human rights, he argues, provide the surest means for achieving this through establishing the political and economic conditions that are conducive to achieving peace and stability. Systematic domestic and international human rights abuses are thereby presented as destabilising phenomena, which states do not have an ultimate interest in. The sovereign nation-state need not be by-passed or ignored. Indeed, Mullerson's argument places the sovereign nation-state at the core of a revised global system, the end of which remains promoting national interests but formulating these interests in a manner which extends to include all nation-states and their populations.

Mullerson's account offers, I believe, a promising basis upon which to develop the engagement with the state that I am proposing. As it stands, it is not wholly satisfactory, however. Thus, his argument has a decidedly Hobbesian character as a consequence of its prioritisation of peace and stability and its appeal to prudential self-interest. Any such account is vulnerable to the enduring 'free-rider' problem, i.e. the interest that a non-compliant state may have in every other state playing by the rules which the dissident state systematically flouts (Arrow, 1963). It is also vulnerable to the inevitable conflict of interests within a single state where the export of arms significantly contributes to the economic wealth of that country whilst providing the means for warfare and instability abroad. These and other concerns will need to be effectively engaged with, both theoretically and practically. Despite their vulnerability to partial interests, human rights remain the most legitimate means for pursuing this task. The obstacles which confront this task testify to how potentially transformative human rights are. They all serve to contradict the complacent assumption that the globe is now generally in thrall to the spirit of human rights. In the theoretical domain the pursuit of this task ought to begin with a critical reformulation and re-characterisation of the nation-state. We must ask what, after all, does the nation-state consist of; what does this entity reduce to ultimately? Human rights advocates are bound to answer in terms which emphasise the lives and well-being of individual human beings. The current legal and political organisation of global politics tends to reify the state and accord each state a legal identity which is unduly separated from those whose lives provide each state's principal resource. Thus, a commitment to human rights as the means for preventing systematic and significant human suffering must reconfigure the state as a means to realising this end and countering the general tendency to recognise the power of those who do not share this commitment. This will require the further strengthening and consolidation of international and cross-border institutions and mechanisms. However, this end should not be pursued with an unduly one-dimensional understanding of the modern nation-state.

CONCLUSION

This chapter has addressed a misunderstanding of the role of the nation-state in protecting human rights. The nation-state remains the single worst violator of human rights, and is aided in this by the current global political framework which, despite proclamations of support for human rights, prioritises partial self-interest over adherence to cosmopolitan values. I have argued that the nation-state retains significant power, despite globalising forces. Rather than seek to ignore or condemn the nation-state, I have argued for the need constructively to engage with nation-states in the attempt to establish a sufficient respect for human rights. This will prove a truly formidable task, testifying to the extent to which we do not live in a human rights age. I have proposed that one approach human rights supporters should take concerns how self-interest is conceptualised and pursued. Ultimately, this task requires a detailed engagement with the issue of political legitimacy and the relationship between human rights and democracy. This is the focal point of the following chapter.

5. Democracy and human rights

INTRODUCTION

The previous chapter examined the role of the nation-state in the realm of human rights. Against a view which represents the state as primarily incompatible with defending human rights, I argued for the need to engage with the state in an attempt to direct resources towards protecting, rather than ignoring or even violating, human rights. As it stands, this request may seem unduly vague or optimistic to some. What is clearly further required is a more detailed account of a state model which is capable of realising and supporting human rights principles and aspirations. This chapter aims to provide just such an account. In keeping with the orientation of the rest of this book, I aim to provide an account capable of realising and supporting human rights principles and aspirations by critically engaging with what appears as a basic misunderstanding of the relationship between the state and human rights. A question typically posed in human rights circles is which kind of state is most compatible with the demands of human rights. The unanimous answer is a democratic state, of course. Democracy and human rights have come to be seen as practically synonymous and identical. In actual fact, they are not. Or, rather, one must say that the relationship between the two is somewhat more complex than the standard answer would suggest. A clear and precise formulation of one's fundamental concepts is of utmost importance in providing a credible and defensible argument in support of the necessity of democracy for human rights. Different and competing understandings of both democracy and human rights infect this area of discussion and debate. This chapter will engage with a sample of these. In particular, I shall critically analyse the claim that democracy consists of the majority expressing its will through popularly mandated legislative authorities and requires nothing more than the protection of civil and political rights for its satisfactory establishment and expression. The realisation of this view of the democratic state is characterised by an impoverished account of human rights. It is also a view which practically endangers the spirit of democracy itself. This chapter, therefore, will argue that democracy and human rights are essential for one another and will defend a substantive account of both which seeks to avoid the pitfalls and limitations that afflict the particular misunderstanding I am here concerned with.

IN SEARCH OF DEMOCRACY

The quintessential view of the nature of the relationship between human rights and democracy is perfectly captured by the 1993 Vienna Declaration, which states that human rights and democracy are 'interdependent and mutually supportive'. As a statement of purpose such pronouncements have a function, but as a purported description of a state of affairs they are positively unhelpful and even misrepresentative. The principal problem concerns how one understands both concepts. What precisely is 'democracy' and what kind of account of human rights is it so compatible with? The remainder of this section addresses this first question, while the second will be answered only at the end of this chapter.

The spectre of nominalism haunts many attempts to understand democracy. Judging by the pronouncements of sovereign states, the world is full of democracies. The term extends to cover bewilderingly different internal political arrangements, from constitutional monarchies to veritably authoritarian republics. The sheer range of political systems which lay claim to the title of 'democracy' raises serious questions over whether the term has any real substance or justifiable basis at all. Presenting a credible account of the relationship between human rights and democracy will require overcoming this particular 'buzzing and booming confusion' (to paraphrase the American Nineteeth Century philosopher, William James) through the identification of some essential elements or components of a genuinely democratic system. A normative commitment to human rights will require going beyond a more overtly politically scientific quantification of those systems which lay claim to being 'democratic' in order to establish what 'being democratic' is legitimately based upon in the first place. As a necessary exercise in normative political analysis this is no easy task.

The task requires the identification and defence of a set of elements or components which may be legitimately said to characterise a democratic system. The purpose of this task is to distinguish between bogus and legitimate democracies. The context for this task is given, in this instance, by a normative commitment to human rights, which, in my terms, entails the elimination of all forms of systematic human suffering so that each and every individual human being enjoys a broadly equal opportunity to lead a minimally good life. Some political theorists have argued that the very attempt to identify the *essence* of democracy is an ultimately futile intellectual project. Starting from an initial premise that all comprehensible human reality ultimately reduces to linguistic phenomena, the philosopher W.B. Gallie presented a series of arguments which sought to identify concepts that are primarily evaluative in character. Gallie coined the term *essentially contested concepts* to refer to concepts which defy any singular and essential definitional properties. Terms such as beauty and truth are concepts which may possess relatively well-defined propositional criteria but the meaning of which is nevertheless the subject of fundamental disagreement and dispute amongst well-intentioned interlocutors. Our meaningful realities comprise elements the meaning of which is fundamentally in dispute. This dispute cannot ultimately be settled by appeal to ostensibly 'objective' and material properties, since our access to any such reality is mediated by a necessarily and unavoidably linguistic representation of 'reality'. We come to view and understand the world through the linguistic terms which prevail in the communities we grow up within. Different communities exhibit different linguistic representations of their surrounding realities and conditions. There is no meta-language or discourse which would allow for these differences being translated into a common discourse. The myth of the Tower of Babel really does testify to the separation of communities and there would appear to be no way back to some essential or pristine linguistic representation of human reality.

Gallie's concept, and with it his philosophical heritage, has been more recently taken up by the political theorist William Connolly (1993). Connolly has directly applied the term to the study of democracy as a political concept. In keeping with Gallie's understanding, Connolly has argued that democracy should be understood and analysed as an essentially contested concept. This is a highly significant claim. Connolly argues that there is no singly correct definition or conception of democracy. One cannot, therefore, settle disputes over what constitutes 'genuine' democracy by appeal to a single, ultimate definition or set of criteria. The existence of a wide range of very different understandings of a single concept like democracy indicates something important about the very nature of the concept; that it lacks a single, ultimate substance or essence. Gallie's insight and Connolly's application of it have been extended to cover a whole range of politically important evaluative concepts beyond democracy, including freedom, the rule of law and sovereignty.

This approach has gained its supporters and adherents in recent years. Ironically perhaps, many appear to discern within it a more 'democratic' approach or spirit to engaging with political differences and the confrontation with hegemonic communities. Connolly's work is exemplary in this regard. That is to say, Connolly has long been opposed to the imposition of élite hegemonic 'realities' which serve to suppress or de-legitimise more local forms of thought and custom. He is best described, then, as taking a pluralist stance on issues of political value. However, a characterisation of democracy as lacking any essential and ultimately defensible elements or criteria runs the very real risk of throwing the baby out with the proverbial bath-water. Connolly's refusal to endorse any ostensibly essential elements of genuine democracy aligns him with those deliberative democrats who are similarly concerned with the manner in which a system comes to be characterised as 'democratic' (see

Gutmann & Thompson, 1996). The concern here is to prevent the usurpation of others' voices through one constituency's appeal to the language of nature or essence. Such appeals are seen as intending towards restricting the scope of deliberation through representing others' views as contrary to nature or reality. The concern is, therefore, primarily directed towards the procedures of political systems and the advocacy of an approach which, by refusing to attempt to 'pin down' political reality to a single representational mode, is considered to be thereby more 'democratic' and worthy of our approval. The danger here lies in the approach's quintessentially abstract and formalistic methodology being unable adequately to substantiate the overtly normative ambition of the approach: its vision rebounds upon itself so as to undermine even the vaguest of definitions of what democracy 'really' consists of. The approach succumbs to the same fate as the cultural relativist who claims that cultural relativism is an independently desirable phenomenon. A commitment to human rights is, as I have argued previously, a commitment to critically evaluating existing human realities from a distinct and normatively substantive standpoint. Justifying this standpoint will require the ability to distinguish between, for example, those forms of 'democracy' which, crudely put, stifle human well-being and those which enhance it. This, in turn, requires the delineation of an account of what constitutes 'genuine' democracy which is capable of over-coming a mere capitulation to the abstract formalism which affects a refusal to make any such distinction. Human rights advocates must define 'democracy', despite the difficulty of the exercise. Our search for the definitional criteria continues.

Those who view democracy in essentially contested terms draw some support from the simple fact that within academic literature, as well as actually existing political systems, there exist a range of different manifestations and formulations of the term. Until relatively recently, a particularly influential perspective was based upon what might be termed a 'negative' account of those rights that were considered essential for citizens to possess within a democratic system. Thus, the political theorists Maurice Cranston (1973) and Robert Nozick (1974) both presented accounts of the democratic state in terms that emphasised the presumed sufficiency of civil and political rights and conceived of these rights claims in overtly negative terms.

In their respective ways, Cranston and Nozick presented an account of political legitimacy which accorded a central place to the role of human rights within a legitimately democratic state. However, their conception of 'human rights' was based upon an overt prioritisation of civil and political rights over their economic, social and cultural counterparts. The logic underlying this position is, initially at least, clear enough to see. Democracy is conceived of as a purely political and civil concern. Democratic states are based upon a principle of formal equality and comprehensive suffrage. Periodic elections need to be held, and they need to be free and fair to the extent that each citizen has a formally equal opportunity to cast their vote for a sufficient range of political candidates. The human rights required to realise these conditions are, on this view, relatively modest. For both Cranston and Nozick these rights must also be restricted to imposing merely negative duties upon others which ensure that individuals' opportunity to participate in the political process is not unduly restricted. Nozick took this perspective further in arguing that legitimate political systems were also based upon an individual's fundamental (negative) right to private property. The fruits of an individual's labour and investments must not be diminished or appropriated through state action in the form of, most obviously, redistributive taxation. For Nozick, the scope of the legitimate state was to be set by individuals' fundamental rights to life, liberty and property. Conceiving of these rights in negative terms served to impose significant constraints upon what a democratically legitimate state could do and provide. Put simply, Nozick viewed the relationship between democracy and these fundamental rights as issuing in a broadly minimal state which refrained from presuming to know what was best for its citizens and desisted from appropriating private wealth as a means for pursuing public goals.

While this approach to democracy is potentially consistent with a number of different ostensibly democratic political systems, it is often associated with a so-called Schumpeterian model of democratic decision-making, after the political theorist Joseph Schumpeter. Schumpeter (1954) argued that democratic decision-making was largely restricted to and was the affair of established political élites, comprising what has subsequently become referred to as the 'political class'. This community comprises elected representatives, party officials and paid civil servants. In effect, the electorate delegates its political responsibility to this specialised class of other citizens whose business is government. In between periodic elections, the process of government largely occurs without the direct involvement or participation of 'ordinary' citizens. Democratic systems differ from their non-democratic counterparts not so much in how politics proceeds, but rather to the extent that within democratic systems the élite political class have to receive a mandate from the electorate: the non-democratic counterparts do not, and thus typically lack the developed framework of civil and political rights found within democratic systems.

Combining the two approaches outlined above, we derive a vision of democracy as largely, if not entirely, based upon the negative protection and promotion of a relatively limited range of civil and political rights. Citizens have an opportunity to stand for political office (even though only a very few ever will) and, more importantly, to cast their votes in periodically held free and fair elections. Once a political party has received a mandate from the electorate through success in a competitive election, it may legitimately pursue those policies upon which it stood for office. The subsequent constraints and limitations of its power are set by the need to respect a relatively minimal range of fundamental human rights. This is a vision of democracy which will be familiar to many and has been particularly influential within the United States. However, is it capable of satisfying the requirements of human rights? Can one achieve complementarity between human rights and democracy by restricting one's account of both?

The Schumpeterian element of this vision of democracy raises particularly pronounced issues for a commitment to human rights, even when one restricts one's focus to largely civil and political rights. The problem may be referred to as 'majoritarianism' and demonstrates the extent to which human rights may still be in jeopardy even within nominally 'democratic' political systems. I shall explain.

Schumpeter's model of democracy is not alone in allowing for an account of democracy which requires little more than the periodic holding of free and fair elections. Political parties and candidates compete for office, and those who achieve the greatest support from the electorate achieve state power for the term of their office. How the 'greatest support' is measured and what the length of the term of office may be vary significantly across nation-states but are formally well-established. Securing democratic legitimacy in this way enables the victorious party or candidate to pursue the mandate given them by the electorate. However, as it stands, this model's very lack of further substantive criteria creates a potentially very real problem for human rights and, with it, for democracy itself. The criteria identified would currently exclude the likes of China, North Korea and even Zimbabwe. The criteria would, however, be satisfied by a large number of otherwise very diverse countries spanning the north and south and east and west segments of the globe. However, if one asks nothing more of democracy than this, one leaves the door wide open for human rights abuses to occur within ostensibly democratic societies.

Political systems which allocate all or the greatest part of political power to those who achieve a majority of the electorate's support are classified as majoritarian systems. The United Kingdom is a majoritarian system, as are many other democratic countries. However, if no other safeguards are established the rights of those who do not support the ruling party or are not aligned with the opposition are potentially at risk within majoritarian systems. Many political scientists and most political activists view politics as an interest-based exercise: agents define and identify their interests and the political 'game' provides the mechanism through which these interests are pursued, if not always realised. Most political systems and most societies comprise diverse constituencies the diversity of which is defined, in part, by their competing interests. In such a context, a government which is elected by a majority of the population may have no overt political interest in upholding the interests of those who do not support it. Indeed, depending upon the extent and depth of the division, the democratically elected government may have a positive interest in promoting the interests of its supporters at the expense of its opponents. Where these interests concern fundamental attributes of human wellbeing, the ensuing action is likely to constitute human rights abuse. Protecting the human rights of all citizens becomes veritably 'irrational' in terms of crude political interest. There are all too many examples of this actually occurring. Enduring post-conflict tensions in the Balkans and parts of Africa provide obvious examples. While this may not extend to the level of human rights abuse, one can also see a similar phenomenon occurring in Belgium. Examples such as these ultimately reduce to disputes concerning what constitutes an integral nation. However, similar issues arise even within far more 'secure' national communities. The division here typically concerns not so much national or ethnic characteristics, but religious or ideological elements. This is most apparent within countries such as the United States and the United Kingdom and the reaction of both countries to the recent terrorist atrocities perpetrated there. Both Human Rights Watch and Amnesty International have documented a growing suspicion of and hostility towards particular minorities or categories of people amongst the wider electorate of both countries. This has been reflected, to some extent, in legislation, such as the two Patriot Acts in the United States and anti-terror legislation in the United Kingdom. Guantanamo Bay continues to function despite the US Supreme Court and has not, needless to say, figured very prominently in the recent US presidential elections. Nations have a basic right to defend and protect themselves. Governments owe a duty of security to their citizens as a basic human right. However, this duty must obviously be maintained in a way that does not itself amount to a systematic human rights abuse, irrespective of how electorally popular such policies and actions may be (Elster, 1993).

In situations of national, ethnic, religious or ideological conflict and division democratically elected governments have acted to restrict and curtail civil and political rights of some of their citizens with the support of those who elected them. In these circumstances, the civil and political human rights of minorities have been subject to abuse and violation within otherwise democratic political systems. Simply stated, democracy and human rights are not, therefore, necessarily synonymous. As stated, they are not interdependent and mutually supportive. A government which wields power only as a result of a freely and fairly held election may, nevertheless, still legally pursue policies which aim at or result in the restriction and violation of minority rights. This has occurred (and is occurring) in developed and developing world societies. For the moment, one may accept Michael Freeman's (2002:72) claim when he writes that democracy is concerned with *who* wields political authority, whereas human rights are concerned with *how* political authority is exercised.

The discussion above has restricted the understanding of human rights to overtly civil and political rights. Torture, violations of habeas corpus, prolonged detention without access to legal representation are all breaches of civil and political rights. One can, however, add further weight to the claim that human rights and democracy are not necessarily mutually supportive and interdependent by extending one's assessment of a capacity for exercising one's democratic rights to include economic, social and cultural factors too. This directly addresses the second concern for those who advocate democracy as based upon and only requiring citizens' possession of negatively enshrined civil and political rights. This concern contains two elements: a critique of any negative inscription of rights and recognition of the facilitative function of economic, social and cultural rights. When combined, these two elements point to a far more holistic understanding of human rights, which seeks to overcome an unduly reified vision of human rights which mistakes merely analytical distinctions for substantive differences. It also provides the basis for establishing an account of democracy which is far more supportive of and consistent with human rights principles.

To possess a negative right is to be said to be free from some particular external constraint or interference. No other agent has positively to do anything for an individual to possess a negative right. On the contrary, the emphasis here is on some other agent *not* doing anything. While it need not necessarily follow, many formulations of human rights in primarily negative terms seek to defend a broadly minimal account of the state. The legitimacy of the state is based upon the protection of a limited collection of fundamental human rights, and conceiving of these rights in negative terms requires far less of the state than if they were conceived of in more overtly positive terms which require more extensive action on the part of the state. This combination of an account of negative rights and a minimal state is, arguably, most apparent in Robert Nozick's political philosophy. However, the weaknesses in the negative conception of human rights are obvious and manifest, quite apart from a more overt dispute over the basis and scope of state power. As civil and political entities, human rights are institutional mechanisms for securing a certain set of conditions. As such, they depend upon and require the establishment of an institutional framework. Creating and maintaining such a framework will require positive action being undertaken and cannot arise simply from a commitment to non-interference. Recognising the need for a minimal state may be construed as an acceptance of this point. However, the argument extends further. Some of the fundamental civil and political rights can be perceived and understood in broadly negative terms. Thus, a right to be free *from* torture looks like a quintessential negative right. Likewise, a right to life may be similarly construed as satisfied by others refraining from seeking to take one's life away. While such rights do have negative dimensions, their realisation takes them firmly into the positive realm, where others have a positive duty to establish and protect the conditions necessary for the exercise of these rights. Take torture, for example. Ensuring that individuals are free from torture will require, amongst other things, educating law enforcement officers in what constitutes torture and how it must be prevented. It will require the establishment of means of judicial overview to ensure that apparent breaches of the right will be investigated and prevented. Neither of these can be secured by a mere commitment to non-interference. This is even more apparent in the case of a right to life. Life is, to coin a term from Charles Taylor (1989), an 'exercise concept'. That is to say, having a life has value only to the extent that one is capable of doing things. A right to life must, therefore, provide adequate support for the exercise of life. This will require being free from physical violation and systematic threats to one's security. It will also require the provision of services that are essential for the opportunity to secure a basic quality of life: education, health-care services, a habitable environment and many of the basic freedoms. These are all positive elements which are necessary for anyone to be said satisfactorily to enjoy a right. Human rights are institutionally enshrined mechanisms which we enjoy only to the extent that we are able to exercise them. An account of human rights in purely negative terms ultimately fails to the extent that it fails to pay sufficient attention to the need to establish and maintain a distinct institutional context which goes beyond a mere insistence that others simply refrain from interfering in others' lives. It also fails to the extent that it must ignore an essential feature of human agency. Even the most apparently 'negative' rights, such as a right to be free from torture and a right to life, must extend to include recognition of the extent to which both, but particularly the latter, entail the provision of conditions for their exercise. Take these conditions away and the very possibility of enjoying these rights is fundamentally jeopardised: as means for seeking to ensure that human beings are capable of leading a minimally good life, human rights necessarily include a significant positive dimension. This insight extends further to the need to overcome the basic distinction conventionally drawn between civil and political rights and their economic, social and cultural counterparts.

The distinction between the two 'categories' of human rights is well established. Typically, authors will point to the different historical trajectories of the two and point out that the former are historically 'older' than the latter (see Ishay, 2004). In addition, it is claimed that the two categories of rights reflect different underlying ideological perspectives, which were manifest during the Cold War and the differences between an ostensibly socialist political bloc which emphasised economic welfare and equality over democratic participation and a liberal-capitalist bloc of nations which were characterised, to a greater or lesser extent, as doing precisely the opposite. While the distinction may have proved useful as an analytical device, it has little merit as a

purported account of human rights *per se*. More specifically, achieving a credible and defensible account of democracy will require overcoming a tendency
to diminish or even ignore the function of economic, social and cultural rights
for the establishment and maintenance of democratic political systems which
are supportive of human rights.

In recent years, a number of theorists have argued that the establishment
and maintenance of democratic political systems require the promotion and
protection of *both* civil and political and economic, social and cultural rights
(Beetham, 1999; Held, 2006; Sen, 1999a; Shue, 1996). The political theorist
David Beetham has provided arguably the most extensive defence of this
particular claim and warrants a detailed analysis here. Beetham argues that
genuinely democratic systems require the protection and promotion of certain
social and economic conditions. He fundamentally challenges the strict
cultural division between civil and political and social and economic rights.
As evidence in support of his claim he argues that in order for any individual
to be said adequately to enjoy the opportunity of political participation (a
civil and political right) they must be free from conditions of crippling ill-
health and abject poverty and have received sufficient education in how the
political system actually works (all social and economic rights). Any individual's sufficiently effective participation in the civil and political affairs of
their country's democratic system requires their possession of sufficient
social and economic resources. Thus, gross disparities in the distribution of
social and economic resources can and do harm democracy. Having a
genuine, rather than a merely formal or token, opportunity to exercise one's
civil and political rights requires a sufficient protection and promotion of
social and economic resources necessary to this end. Because human rights
aims at establishing the conditions necessary for securing a minimally good
life this does not mean that everyone must have the same income and
resources. It does however commit the state to pursuing redistributionist policies to secure that disparities in income and resources are not so great as
systematically to disadvantage the least well-off. The terms of Beetham's
argument bear some resemblance to John Rawls's (1971) theory of justice
insofar as both argue that a commitment to liberty and equality commits the
state to ensuring that even the least well-off are sufficiently well endowed to
be able to exercise all of their rights when the need arises. On this view both
absolute and relative poverty are viewed as fundamentally important to an
assessment of how democratic a country can be said to be. In essence,
Beetham argues that the protection and promotion of democracy require the
adequate protection of both civil and political and social and economic rights.
The latter are presented as essential prerequisites for democracy, as an essential condition for democracy is the ability of each citizen adequately to exercise his or her civil and political rights. Beetham's claims received

independent support from the economist Amartya Sen (1999a) who has provided a detailed analysis of development as comprising both civil and political and economic, social and cultural constituents. Sen (1981) has also added weight to this general approach in his demonstration that famines do not occur within sufficiently democratic societies: the positive exercise of civil and political rights is presented as enjoying, at the very least, a positive correlation with the enjoyment of fundamental economic, social and cultural rights. This general approach amounts to a form of what Henry Shue (1996) has referred to as rights holism. From this perspective, human rights are mutually supportive and interdependent (to paraphrase the language of the Vienna Declaration). Possessing and exercising any fundamental human right cannot be abstracted from the possessing and exercising of any other fundamental human right. Possessing a sufficient opportunity to participate in the democratic affairs of one's political community entails the enjoyment of a sufficient level of material wellbeing. The extent to which one's material wellbeing is adequately secured is itself inherently affected by the extent of one's opportunity to influence civil and political decision-making. A concern for establishing democratic conditions which are genuinely consistent with human rights generally therefore requires a concern for both categories of human rights as part of a holistic vision of rights as an integral whole.

Rights holism is not accepted by everyone (see Kukathas, 2003). Beetham's argument in particular is clearly incompatible with the views considered earlier in this chapter. Thus, in strictly empirical terms his account would appear to serve to limit the claims that societies such as the United States, Brazil or India can make to the title of democracy, given the gross disparities of wealth found within all of those societies. It also has very tangible implications for the ideological basis of institutions such as the World Bank and the WTO which are committed, to differing degrees, to a view of the primacy of the market.[1] To some, Beetham's argument may look like an attempt to load the dice in favour of welfare-state-based countries for any democratic audit. If you hold that rights are best understood in negative terms, you will also be inclined to reject Beetham's argument as demanding too much of rights. In order adequately to analyse and evaluate the strength of Beetham's version of rights holism we will need to broaden our scope and consider his more ambitious attempt to identify an account of human rights and democracy capable of overcoming the problems we have considered to this point.

---

[1]   The role of the market in the global human rights sphere is the subject of the next chapter.

RECONCILING DEMOCRACY AND HUMAN RIGHTS

Beetham rejects the two accounts of democracy we have considered so far. He explicitly rejects the view that democracy is devoid of any objective and defining criteria. In addition, he also rejects the view that democracy can be sufficiently secured by the establishment of largely negative civil and political rights alone. More generally, he argues that no country is completely democratic and no country is completely undemocratic. Thus he envisages democracy as referring to a spectrum, rather than an either/or type of arrangement. Democracy itself, he insists, is founded upon two core ideals or components. These are popular control and political equality. Beetham states that 'control by citizens over their collective affairs and equality between citizens in the exercise of that control are the basic democratic principles' (Beetham, 1999: 91). A country is more democratic to the extent that it protects and promotes these ideals and less democratic to the extent that it frustrates and obstructs these ideals. These both constitute the core elements of democracy which, as such, enable us to provide evaluative criteria for the term. Taken together these elements also entail the sufficient realisation of economic and social conditions as prerequisites for the exercise of democracy. I agree with Beetham's account to this point. Defending this claim, however, requires a closer analysis of what he understands by popular control and political equality.

Popular control ultimately derives its value from the ideal of individual liberty we considered in a previous chapter. Democracy provides the political means by which each individual citizen may actively participate in and seek to influence the political affairs and decisions of the community to which he or she belongs. Democracy provides the framework through which each individual citizen, singly or in association with others, can become an agent, rather than simply a passive recipient of other people's actions and decisions. In essence popular control consists of the rule of the people. Political legitimacy and authority emanate from the electorate via a variety of institutional mechanisms, principal among which are periodic free and fair elections. Each individual citizen may not achieve exactly what he or she wants through participation in this process, but through participation they ensure that their voice is heard. Popular control may be contrasted with a system of benign dictatorship where decisions are made by a single, unelected body or individual allegedly in the interests of those who are governed and which is not accountable or answerable to the people. In democracies political authority emanates not from God, nor from an alleged greater insight into what is good for us, but from the people.

On the face of it, popular control is not sufficient to satisfy the requirements for genuine democracy. Most obviously, a sole concern for rule by the people leaves open the possibility of majoritarian governments pursuing repressive policies against particularly unpopular minorities, who had an opportunity to have their voice heard, so to speak, but in losing the election now face a politically empowered opponent. What is therefore required is a means of evaluating popular control in order to ensure that equality extends beyond the day of the election to include both how votes are to be weighted and, perhaps more importantly, how each citizen will be treated by the political authorities more generally. Beetham includes political equality as one of his central elements of democracy to ensure that a democratic system accords each and every citizen a formally equal legal and moral standing. Each individual is to count for one and for no more than one. In a democratic system, clever people or economically prosperous people are not to be given additional votes, say, over their less intelligent or prosperous counterparts. They may and often do gain far greater political influence over decisions which affect us all, but this is not to be grounded in any formal allocation of political status. This notion has been absolutely central to the political campaigns of constituencies of people who have been (and may continue to be) discriminated against by the political system to which they are exposed. However, Beetham's inclusion of equality as one of the two core elements of democracy is meant to extend beyond simply regulating the electoral process. For Beetham, equality extends beyond the ballot box, so to speak, to determine how individual citizens are to be treated more generally by the political authorities of a human rights respecting democratic state.

The equality ideal is undeniably central to the human rights doctrine. In according the ideal such prominence in his own account of democracy, Beetham necessarily draws upon a more comprehensive conception of the ideal. This appeal is not as simple as it may at first appear. The equality ideal is an internally complex notion which has attracted a great deal of attention. Indeed, it would be correct to say that there is a vast literature on the subject of equality as a moral, political and legal ideal (Dworkin, 1986; Sen, 1981). Typically, the literature distinguishes between two forms of equality: 'natural' equality and conventional (or social) equality. Natural measures of equality concern purportedly purely physical and environmental factors and conditions. In contrast, conventional equality is concerned with cultural and social factors and conditions. Our concern here is, needless to say, with the latter. The equality ideal holds, at its core, that all individual human beings are to be considered as possessing an equal moral standing: all human beings are of equal moral value and, as such, deserve to be treated as morally equal. The equality ideal appeals to the most abstract attributes of the human condition and human agency, which are most typically conceived of in the form of a capacity for reason. The abstract character of the ideal also represents one of its principal weaknesses, or stress points. In actuality, human beings are not equal when judged by their enjoyment of material resources or influence over

the affairs of their community. The world is actually more accurately characterised as beset by deep inequalities in these regards. Indeed, a significant part
of the very impetus for human rights consists of a response to existing inequality. Beetham's account of equality has normative force as a call for how conditions must be if a particular state is to be considered genuinely democratic in
terms which are acceptable to a commitment to human rights principles.

It is important to be clear what is understood by 'equality' here. The existence of gross inequalities is typically viewed as evidence of the ideal's denial
and frustration. Some might thereby conceive of the ideal as requiring a form
of so-called radical egalitarianism, which is most typically associated with
Marxism. Beetham's conception of the equality ideal does not require this. A
genuinely democratic system does not, for example, require the elimination of
disparities in wealth and income. Relative wealth and relative poverty will
exist within human rights respecting democratic systems. However, a commitment to equality as a fundamental attribute of the political status and standing
of each citizen does require the establishment of conditions which facilitate
and support this. If the disparities in wealth become so great as significantly
to undermine the poorer citizens' access to the political institutions of the
community, for example, then the inclusion of equality as a core element of
genuine democracy will require the state taking some corrective action.
Similarly, if certain individuals are discriminated against on the basis, not so
much of their poverty but their identity, this constitutes a violation of the
equality principle and will require state action if these individuals' human
rights are not to be adversely affected.

Beetham's understanding of the equality principle goes beyond that which
informs the work of writers such as Nozick and Cranston. A mere proclama-
tion that everyone starts from a broadly equal position and possesses a merely
abstract form of equality typically ignores the extent to which subsequent
material and social conditions may significantly undermine some individuals'
continuing enjoyment of the equality ideal. However, his account does not
take human rights into the Marxist domain which (on the conventional reading) seeks to eradicate all substantive distinctions and differences within a
single political community. Taking Beetham's understanding as representative
of human rights' conception of the equality ideal we may say that human rights
stands half-way between the libertarianism of Nozick and the radical egalitarianism of Marx. The human rights doctrine is not opposed to the existence of
all and any forms of income inequality or inequalities of outcome, as they are
typically labelled. Nor is the doctrine committed to a view of individuals as
devoid of identity. Rather, the human rights view of equality is concerned to
ensure the establishment of a particular form of equality which can allow for
disparities of wealth, resources and identities. Thus, human rights is committed to a view of equality which holds that all should be equal before the law

and that all human beings are entitled to enjoy a sufficient degree of respect and concern irrespective of their social, religious, ethnic or national identities and commitments. The crucial test here concerns whether each individual enjoys broadly equal freedom from systematic and significant human suffering and broadly equal opportunity to influence the fundamental decisions made which affect their lives.

As stated, human rights and democracy are not necessarily mutually supportive and interdependent. A commitment to human rights entails the assimilation of particular criteria within any democratic audit of a single nation-state. Most importantly, if human rights and democracy are to enjoy a genuinely supportive co-existence, the ideal of popular control must be complemented by political equality. In Beetham's terms this will require the establishment of conditions which genuinely ensure that material and cultural differences do not adversely restrict any individual's sufficient equality. A commitment to the equality principle serves to place constraints and limitations upon what governments may do. It will also, at times, serve to direct positive government action in ways which may not always be popular with those sections of the electorate who supported the government in the first place. The contour and direction of this argument should be sufficiently clear. However, while it is an argument I believe to be worthy of support, it does raise some interesting issues and questions which need to be addressed before concluding on the relationship between human rights and democracy.

IMPLICATIONS AND CONSEQUENCES

In turning towards a concern for how the model I have been supporting and outlining may be institutionally realised one is confronted by a number of potential implications and consequences. Three questions are particularly salient: what relationship is envisaged here between civil and political and economic and social rights? What role, if any, does the judiciary have to play in protecting human rights within democratic systems? Finally, what status should be accorded to so-called collective rights claims in this context? I shall consider each in turn.

The first question received an indirect answer earlier in this chapter. By way of reminder, I argued that democracy should be understood as an institutional process which is dependent upon sufficient numbers of citizens being sufficiently involved in the political process. What precisely constitutes 'sufficient' in both cases will be a moot point and is open to continuing discussion. However, difficulties in securing agreement on such criteria should not provide inadvertent justification for overly disinterested, disengaged or purposefully alienated electorates becoming primarily passive recipients of others' decisions. In this respect, democracy should be understood as an exercise concept. Human rights' emphasis upon the equality ideal requires that every citizen possess a broadly equal opportunity to influence and participate in the political affairs of his or her community. The ability to do so cannot be secured merely through the formal establishment of sufficient civil and political rights. Citizens' exercise of their democratic rights may be obstructed or unduly constrained by factors extraneous to the protective cover provided by these rights. Thus, Beetham argues that the denial or significant diminution of economic and social rights may adversely affect citizens' capacity and opportunity to exercise their civil and political rights. The effects of poverty, chronic ill-health, social and cultural isolation may extend beyond their obvious economic and social spheres adversely to affect the ability of those afflicted to participate in the political process. These conditions may, of course, be themselves largely due to existing forms of civil and political exclusion and discrimination. Overcoming this and restoring a broadly equal and sufficient capacity for civil and political participation will require addressing and overcoming these forms of economic and social deprivation. This may, in turn, require the state to pursue welfare policies which may not be fully supported by the electorate. In cases such as these, the limits of and justification for any such policies should be set by what is required to restore a sufficient opportunity for broadly equal civil and political participation amongst all of those who are subject to the state's jurisdiction.

An argument supportive of the view that civil and political rights and economic and social rights are mutually supportive may take two potential forms. The first holds that civil and political rights are of ultimate importance, and the value of their economic and social counterparts is instrumental to this end. The second holds, by contrast, that both categories of rights are complementary and are better understood as two parts of a single and integral whole. This second view corresponds with Henry Shue's concept of rights holism and is most conducive to the more general account of human rights I have been defending throughout this book. Human rights exist in order to provide a means for evaluating and countering systematic forms of human suffering. Human suffering rarely, if ever, neatly subdivides into two different categories. Human beings suffer as a consequence of gross material deprivation. They may also be exposed to significant and systematic suffering as a consequence of being denied opportunities to participate in the institutions and decisions which afflict their lives. While it may be analytically useful on occasion to distinguish between different categories of human rights, the purpose of the doctrine can only be adequately pursued by a refusal to separate out some forms of human suffering from others. Beetham's account of democracy is valuable precisely to the extent that it refuses to perpetuate an overly one-dimensional account of human rights.

The second question this account of human rights and democracy raises concerns the role of the judiciary in upholding a democratic system's commitment to the equality ideal, in particular. For many, democracy appears to be a concern for politics and the design of political institutions. Textbooks will often refer to distinctions between the executive and the legislature. Typically, it will be argued that democracy requires a separation of powers between the two, and may even require separate legislative assemblies, as exemplified by the US Houses of Congress and the Senate. Absent from this account, however, is the role of the judiciary in upholding a state's human rights commitments. The judiciary has an established role in respect of protecting the constitutions of many states, such as the role played by the Supreme Court in the United States and the House of Lords in the United Kingdom. Differences of opinion exist, however, on the question of the role played by the judiciary in protecting human rights and democracy.

The philosopher Jeremy Waldron (1999) argues against the call to grant regulatory powers to the judiciary within a democratic political system. For Waldron, the judiciary represents an undue and unnecessary constraint upon the will of the people, as expressed through free and fair elections. For him, political participation is an essential human good, a means by which we realise our potential as a species. Bestowing regulatory powers upon the judiciary subverts this good. It also amounts to the establishment of un-, or even anti-, democratic forces within an otherwise democratic society. After all, judges are typically appointed and not elected. Their very independence entails their not being unduly and directly exposed to the electorate or even the legislature. Judges may exercise their role and duties with great care and integrity. However, for Waldron, this will still result in outcomes which are antithetical to genuine democracy. For him, the legitimacy of constitutions, treaties or international human rights instruments is ultimately dependent upon their being subject to validation by the will of the people. Judges should not, therefore, be capable of striking down or rendering illegal laws passed by legislative assemblies. Human rights would appear to represent to Waldron not so much an *a priori* constraint upon what democratic governments may legitimately do, as that which the will of the people should be in a position to approve. Presumably, an enlightened electorate will see no conflict between a commitment to human rights and a commitment to the political community's fundamental interests.

A radically different approach is adopted by Ronald Dworkin (1996). Dworkin argues that a commitment to human rights within a democratic political system can only be secured through granting a sufficient degree of independent power to the judiciary and thereby limiting the competence of the executive and the legislature. In particular, he argues that the commitment to the equality principle is not safe and secure within systems which do not include some sufficiently robust, independent and long-standing checks and balances upon the legislature and the executive. Effectively appealing to the notion that the whole point of human rights is to place limits on how power is exercised so that political power cannot be legitimately exercised in a manner which is hostile to human rights, Dworkin insists that genuinely democratic systems must include an independent judiciary and, in effect, a bill of rights which provides a moral blueprint for the legitimate exercise of political power within a given system. The bill of rights should closely resemble the terms of the International Bill of Rights and the independence of the judiciary requires that judges are not easily manipulated by political pressure and are protected from the electorate. A necessary, though not necessarily sufficient, condition for achieving this is the ratification and implementation of the two covenants of the International Bill of Rights. In addition, Dworkin has generally argued that the task of overseeing and protecting these rights must ultimately lie with an independent judiciary. In this way, protecting human rights is viewed as positively requiring the removal of human rights from the immediate political sphere. It is important to see that this can be achieved within a multitude of different democratic political systems. Thus, the United Kingdom has gone some way to meeting these criteria through the establishment of the Human Rights Act 1998 which, to some extent at least, invests the judiciary with the power to strike down some forms of legislation on the ground that they violate terms of the Act, which is itself significantly influenced by the European Convention on Human Rights. It is interesting to note, however, that the Human Rights Act does not generally enjoy widespread electoral support in the United Kingdom. Advocates of the United States' system of government would point to that country as a good example of the division of powers between the various organs of power in a manner which supports the US Constitution. While it is administered by presidentially appointed judges, the US Constitution does offer some protection against electorally popular violations of the fundamental rights enshrined within the Constitution.

Neither side to this debate possesses a monopoly on wisdom or sound argument. The spectre of unelected judges imposing demands upon the legislature and the executive runs the risk of being unpopular amongst the electorate, and this in turn typically undermines the support enjoyed by human rights principles under these circumstances. On the other hand, the fundamental rights of minorities remain a problem for many ostensibly democratic countries. In many cases, executives and legislatures have proven unwilling or unable to protect the rights of minority constituencies. In this context a commitment to human rights entails a commitment to the equality principle. If politicians prove incapable of securing this ideal, then human rights supporters ought to turn to the judiciary as a potential ally in their cause. This will remain, no doubt, a complex and difficult relationship. Human rights supporters should, I believe, seek to avoid endorsing unduly one-dimensional, either/or types of arguments. In practice, both politicians and the judiciary have an important contribution to make in realising the human rights of all individuals. In this regard, it is important that the democratic culture in such societies is deep and robust enough to allow for significant civic involvement in maintaining sufficient pressure upon all of those charged with the power to promote, rather than frustrate, human rights principles.

The final question for this chapter concerns the status of collective rights claims within sufficiently democratic societies. This is a difficult issue, which has attracted a great deal of attention (Freeman, 1995; Kukathas, 2003; Kymlicka, 1992). As we have seen in the discussion outlined in previous chapters, the dominant tendency within human rights theory has been to conceive of the principal bearer of human rights as the individual, who is typically conceived of in abstract terms and as constitutively devoid of social identity. Advocates of so-called non-western approaches to human rights have challenged this assumption. In recent decades this intellectual challenge has received some recognition in the form of aspects of international human rights law which are more sympathetic towards non-individualistic approaches to human rights. Thus, since the 1980s there has been a whole raft of protocols, conventions and instruments which explicitly identify a given category of human beings as subject to discrimination and inequality precisely because of their identities. Prominent examples are the Convention on the Elimination on all forms of Discrimination Against Women (1981), the Convention Concerning Indigenous and Tribal Peoples in Independent Countries (1989) and the Declaration on the Rights of Persons Belonging to National or Ethnic, Religious or Linguistic Minorities (1993). While all of these instruments continue to operate with a conception of the individual as the principal bearer of human rights, all of them acknowledge the extent to which individuals' particular identities will have a bearing upon their ability to enjoy their rights. None of these, however, should be understood as bestowing collective rights on communities as such.

Some have argued that simply recognising the existence of socially grounded identities does not go far enough to redress the injustices some communities suffer as a direct consequence of others' attitudes towards those communities (Kymlicka, 1989; Young, 1990). On this view, people's well-being is directly affected by the status enjoyed by the community to which they adhere and from which they have largely derived their identities. Communities and cultures which are subject to systematic discrimination, it is argued, are legitimate candidates for possessing rights in their own right. Thus, collective rights to such communal entities as land and language are presented as legitimate objects of collective rights claims. This argument is considered to be bolstered when applied to cultural communities that typically lack a robust account of individual moral sovereignty (Parekh, 2000). Intellectually, this debate involves an enduring clash between two philosophical doctrines: liberalism and communitarianism (Mulhall & Swift, 1992). As a distinct doctrine, human rights has typically enjoyed a much closer relationship to liberalism than to communitarianism. This is most apparent in the status accorded to the morally sovereign individual. Liberals are typically conceived of as necessarily committed to upholding this ideal, even where this commitment may prove damaging or destructive to cultural communities (Barry, 2001). By contrast, communitarians are viewed as bestowing intrinsic value on cultural communities in their own right, so to speak. In reality, the differences between the two are less clear-cut than such analytical distinctions would suggest. However, it would be correct to say that human rights' commitment to the morally sovereign individual is of fundamental importance in determining the legitimacy of collective rights claims. It is unlikely that this will significantly change in the years to come. Determining the extent to which cultural communities may possess rights as such, over and above the heads of their individual members, will remain a difficult topic of discussion and action for human rights supporters. In this respect, two things should remain at the forefront of people's concern. First, that any such rights claims must prove ultimately compatible with the commitment to the equality ideal that is central to both human rights and a genuine account of democracy. Second, that this need not always entail rejecting more communitarian-inclined ethical and political approaches. Democracy requires that individuals have an opportunity to shape and influence the political decisions which influence their lives. At times this may require bolstering the individual against an unduly repressive élite. At other times, it may require demonstrating a greater degree of trust and confidence in ostensibly non-individualistic communities' ability to make equitable and legitimate decisions without undue 'guidance' and interference from those who claim to know better. Once again, this is ultimately a concern for where the line may be legitimately drawn between what is both politically legitimate and sufficiently consistent with the equality ideal. This is an area of human rights theory and practice which remains very much work in progress.[2]

CONCLUSION: BRINGING ENDS TOGETHER

Our approach to the relationship between human rights and democracy must eschew intellectual platitudes or complacent assumptions. This chapter has

---

[2]   See Fagan (2006) for my contribution to this debate. I aim to examine the issue of human rights and cultural diversity in a subsequent volume.

argued, in effect, that one should not believe something to be true simply because it has been declared in a United Nations document. The 1993 Vienna Declaration declares democracy and human rights to be mutually supportive and interdependent. In actuality this is not necessarily so and is rather more complex than the statement would suggest. I have argued that a democratic political system must be achieved if the nation-state is to be directed towards promoting human rights. However, I have sought to clarify precisely what is required for democracy in this regard. A commitment to human rights introduces a set of criteria which have not always been associated with or present within democratic states. Of particular importance are a concern to protect minorities against majority repression and a commitment to the equality ideal. In addition, I have argued that human rights are to be understood in a holistic sense, encompassing both categories of human rights. Reconciling human rights with democracy will require, on this basis, a sufficient concern for promoting both civil and political and economic, social and cultural rights as integral components of a genuinely human rights supporting democratic polity. This entails acknowledging the extent to which a view of democracy as requiring little more than a concern for civil and political rights is to misunderstand human rights results in an attenuated model of democracy. Ultimately, democracy and human rights are not essentially identical and synonymous: democracy is concerned with distributing power and human rights attempt to place limits on how that power can be exercised. A commitment to upholding human rights requires the establishment of political and legal conditions which, in Jack Donnelly's terms, 'requires a very specific kind of government in which the morally and politically prior rights of citizens . . . limit the range of democratic decision-making. Democracy and human rights are mutually reinforcing in contemporary liberal democracies because the competing claims of democracy and human rights are resolved in favour of human rights' (1999: 192).

Donnelly is correct in perceiving a potential divergence between human rights and democracy. However, his insistence that any conflict between the two must be resolved in favour of human rights indicates a threat and a challenge to human rights supporters. The task is to establish and distribute arguments which show that genuinely democratic polities do not provide a mechanism by which majorities may always get their way. A commitment to human rights will, at times, court unpopularity amongst electorates and may even appear to some as a veritable form of political injustice through the restriction of the manifest will of the majority. The cornerstone of the case for human rights in such instances will remain a defence of the equality principle and a reasonable delineation of what constitutes human rights in the first instance. In this respect, however, human rights have a vital contribution to make to protecting democratic systems from the abuse of political power. This will continue to prove to be a difficult task. The difficulty of this task testifies to the extent to which perceiving human rights and democracy as necessarily synonymous is a potentially dangerous misunderstanding in need of remedy.

6. Global economic inequalities and human rights

INTRODUCTION

This chapter focuses upon an enduring misunderstanding concerning the appropriate relationship between human rights and duties. Critics of human rights have argued that the doctrine ultimately promotes selfishly egoistic tendencies within contemporary society. The existence of human rights encourages individuals to demand more and more for themselves with little regard for how these demands may be met or who may be expected to provide for them. The discourse of rights is viewed as complementing an increasingly irresponsible attitude towards society and other human beings (MacIntyre, 1984 and 1988). In stark contrast to their ostensive ambition, human rights serve to enshrine existing inequalities and social deprivation as a consequence of the 'haves' exercising their rights to protect their relative wealth and privilege. This vision of rights has its origins in Marx's (1978) critique of rights as a bourgeois institution which is constitutively incapable of achieving conditions of universal justice for all. This chapter aims to challenge this view. I shall examine the relationship between rights and duties through the very real world scenario of global economic inequalities. In essence, my argument is that the appalling state of global inequality is a consequence, in part, not of the realisation of human rights, but of their denial or distortion. I shall argue that, combined with their universal character, human rights are intrinsically related to correlative and corresponding duties. In keeping with the account of universality I outlined in an earlier chapter, I argue that human rights do not exist, nor can they be justified, within or by appeal to a social vacuum. Human rights are social institutions and concern the quality of social relationships. While the individual remains the distinct subject of human rights, achieving the promise of a world in which all human beings have the opportunity to lead minimally good lives, free from the threat of systematic and significant suffering, can be achieved only as a collective enterprise. Conceiving of human rights in this way entails recognising that duties are intrinsic to rights. After examining the extent of global inequality and considering some of the principal obstacles to overcoming or significantly reducing the extent of inequality, I turn to the question of the role of duty within human rights as a moral discourse and a social institution. I present and defend a particular account of duty as a means for more effectively pursuing the principal end of human rights.

THE EXTENT OF GLOBAL INEQUALITY

Until relatively recently it would have been fair to say that the dominant focus of the human rights community consisted of a concern for the violation of civil and political rights. A corresponding interest in and concern for economic and social rights is a relatively recent and still emerging development. The widely recognised subordinate status of economic and social rights belies the sheer scale and gravity of human rights violations in this sphere. Indeed, any assessment of existing data must conclude that the most systematically and extensively violated human right is the right to an adequate standard of living, nutrition and health enshrined by Article 25 of the Universal Declaration of Human Rights (UDHR). Article 25 holds out the promise of all human beings enjoying a standard of living which is sufficient to protect them from the ravages of famine, poverty, lack of shelter, inadequate sanitation and chronic illness. As a further development of this Article, the International Covenant on Economic, Social and Cultural Rights (ICESCR) provides a far more detailed delineation and formulation of such rights. In reality, these rights are violated each and every day on a truly appalling scale.

Let us be clear. Even in a world facing economic recession and declining economic values there remain more than enough material resources in the world to ensure that each and every human being's basic needs can be met. The greater part of the world's population faces a daily struggle to survive. The following statistics should suffice as an accurate and sufficiently comprehensive measure of the extent and scale of the problem.

- In 2001 46 per cent (2.8 billion people) of the global population were living below the World Bank's $2 a day poverty line.
- 1.2 billion people live on less than $1 a day.
- 18 million people die prematurely from poverty-related causes every year.
- 50,000 people each and every day die from poverty-related causes; of these 34,000 are under the age of 5.
- In contrast, the average income of citizens of affluent countries is fifty times greater in purchasing power than that of our counterparts living in the world's poor countries.
- The assets and wealth of the world's top three billionaires are greater than those of 600 million people living in the least developed countries of the world.

- Economic trends over the past forty years have seen the richer getting richer and the poor getting poorer.

Few people actively endorse such conditions. Few people argue that these figures represent anything other than a moral tragedy. Despite this, the conditions persist. What is worse, global inequality has actually worsened over the last fifteen years, despite a very large increase in total global wealth. During a period in which some theorists have been proclaiming the age of human rights, more and more people have suffered the consequences of an ever greater violation of their basic economic and social rights.

WHAT ARE THE OBSTACLES TO OVERCOMING GLOBAL INEQUALITY?

Assuming the existence of a basic moral intuition that the suffering endured by so many human beings is wrong, we must ask why the conditions persist and are actually getting worse. However, having raised the question, one must immediately acknowledge the complexity of the subject-matter and the difficulties anyone will confront in adequately addressing it. The topic is huge and crosses over many different academic, social, political and even moral domains. The account offered here will be, necessarily, limited. The purpose of this section is, however, to provide a sufficiently detailed and comprehensive perspective upon how others, from various disciplines and positions, have analysed the obstacles to overcoming global inequality. Resorting to the language of 'inequality', rather than, say, 'differences', presupposes a particularly evaluative view of these circumstances: they are morally indefensible. I will consider the arguments of some of those who dispute this characterisation in due course, when I consider the question of establishing a duty to seek to remedy or alleviate the suffering these circumstances testify to. For the time being, though, my characterisation of the obstacles to overcoming global inequality will, no doubt, be influenced by my moral standpoint on this issue.

Whatever one's moral evaluation of the distribution of global wealth, the statistics outlined above are compelling. Any evaluation of them must also include recognition of another fact: there are sufficient material resources in the world to eradicate absolute poverty. The world contains sufficient material resources not to ensure universal happiness (what, after all, would that mean?) but to ensure that every human being has an opportunity to lead a minimally good life in the form of being free from the threat of systematic and significant human suffering. While this might be sometimes difficult ultimately to assess and quantify in respect of any individual's participation in the political affairs of his or her community, its denial is typically far more immediate and recognisable in respect of an individual's basic economic and social rights. The situation is urgent and manifestly ongoing. Accepting that sufficient over-all resources exist to remedy this situation entails a subsequent acceptance of the fact that the issue fundamentally concerns the distribution of these resources: the principal obstacle, then, is not availability of resources, but rather their distribution. So, why are resources distributed in a manner which results in such wholesale denial of countless millions of human beings' funda-mental rights?

As I made clear above, this issue is deeply complex. In order to avoid falling victim to the complexity, it is useful analytically to distinguish between different categories of obstacles and factors in the maintenance of global poverty. Four categories seem particularly pertinent in this regard: the global economic system, institutional factors, social and political conditions, and finally moral beliefs. I shall consider each in turn.

With the demise of the Soviet Union and the corresponding collapse of many centralised, command economies the predominant economic model for global economic relations and exchange is capitalism. It would be foolish to characterise capitalism in terms which suggest that it is a phenomenon with a single essence or manifestation. Definitions and accounts of capitalism vary profoundly in accordance, it seems, with whether it is being approved or disapproved of (see Hayek, 1960; Sen, 1981). Enduring elements include a focus upon the accumulation of surplus capital as the principal motive of capi-talist enterprise and a subordination of the demands of labour to this end. Other elements include the promotion of greater private wealth and a desire to restrict public expenditure. In developing world societies, a transition of economies from primarily command-based to exchange-driven mechanisms has entailed a focus upon the development of more efficient productive tech-nologies, the promotion of cash crops over more traditional forms of produc-tion designed to satisfy the producers' needs, and a significant reduction in state expenditure (Roxborough, 1979). However one defines capitalism and whichever manifestation of it one focuses upon, a clear consensus has formed which views the global economic system as primarily dominated by institu-tions, practices, beliefs, conventions and laws which aim to prioritise the demands of capital over all rival or alternative elements of the global economic system. Put simply, political consensus amongst the most powerful and democratically elected governments in the world has held this to be a good thing. In the developed world and much of the developing world, few politi-cal candidates have successfully campaigned on an overtly anti-capitalist plat-form. Despite capitalism's dominance of the global economic realm, critics do remain. Marxists such as G.A Cohen (1978) and a plethora of anti-globalisa-tion organisations continue to insist that capitalism is an inherently destructive force which seeks to convert all of life into a mere resource for the generation of profit: natural resources are plundered and previously self-sustainable communities are transformed into cogs of a globalising capitalist machine. There are clear beneficiaries of this economic system but there are also very clear victims. Some may be inclined to dismiss the criticisms and claims of Marxists and anti-globalisation organisations purely on the grounds of their overt bias and prejudice. Leaving aside whether this is a legitimate way to counter such approaches, one may turn instead to other critical accounts which do not share the overtly ideological antipathy to capitalism *per se*. A perfect example of one such approach can be found in the work of the philosopher Thomas Pogge (2002).

Pogge's detailed analysis of global capitalism and existing inequalities demonstrates that one does not have to be either a Marxist or an anti-globalisation 'warrior' to hold to the view that the current global economic system is a principal cause of global poverty. Interestingly, Pogge draws heavily upon the philosophy of John Locke (1988). Locke's political philosophy includes and emanates from a defence of private property as an inalienable right of the individual. This is a fundamental component of capitalism and has attracted consistent criticism from those opposed to capitalism (Cohen, 1978; Marx, 1978). From this basis, Pogge proceeds to develop a critique of the contemporary global economic order. He extends the application of the right beyond the confines of a bourgeois class of entrepreneurs and the established affluent societies of the globe and applies it to all peoples everywhere. Pogge argues that the current economic system is a recognisably capitalist system. However, he proceeds to argue that market exchange and people's right to enjoy the fruits of their labour are fundamentally distorted and undermined by the establishment and maintenance of power imbalances within the system. Put simply, he argues that the affluent societies of the globe utilise their economic and political power to secure unfair trading and exchange conditions to the advantage of themselves and their populations. In effect, he argues that existing inequalities are not the consequence of free and fair exchange and trading between nations. On the contrary, global inequality results from the affluent nations' ability to establish monopolies and tariffs which primarily and unduly benefit the powerful at the expense of the powerless. The poor are poor as a consequence of the denial of a genuinely level economic playing field. He claims that the global economic system is arranged continuously to benefit the wealthy at the direct expense of the poor: our wealth is founded upon their poverty. The actions of a vast swathe of economic agents is causing profound harm to our poor counterparts: we misappropriate their wealth and resources to our ends. The world contains very affluent and very poor people. The actions of the affluent are a direct cause of the misery of the poor, misery which consists, in large part, of the fundamental and systematic violation of their human rights. He writes:

The affluent Western states are no longer practicing slavery, colonialism, or genocide. But they still enjoy crushing economic, political, and military dominance over
the rest of the world. And a large proportion of humankind can still barely obtain
enough to survive. (2002: 6)

Pogge's critique of the contemporary global economic order is interesting
to the extent that it is not motivated by an ideological aversion to individual
private property rights, nor is he obviously opposed to capitalism as a framework in which individuals' rights to free and fair economic exchange can
potentially occur. His account places significant emphasis upon negative
rights and duties as a means for achieving economically just and fair global
conditions. These rights are systematically violated, according to Pogge, as a
direct consequence of the misappropriation of others' wealth which results
from the political manipulation of the principal global regulatory institutions,
such as the WTO and the World Bank. Pogge is not alone in pursuing this line
of criticism and in his targeting the global financial organisations' distorting
effect upon trade and exchange (see Sachs, 2005).

Pogge's critique is vulnerable to criticism, however. His appeal to a
Lockean account of entitlement to private property appears, in the light of
the development of literature in this field, a little naïve and unduly simplis-
tic (see Becker, 2000). One may also point to the relative lack of engagement
in his work with some of the more quintessential advocates of global capitalism in its current form (Luttwak, 1999; Westbrook, 2004). Despite such
potential criticisms, his analysis is detailed and comprehensive. It also
emerges from a clear sympathy with the spirit of promoting equal individual
liberty, which capitalism so often evokes but which current global circumstances so clearly defy. Most importantly, his critique of capitalism may be
taken as illustrative to the extent that it coincides with and draws upon
demonstrable empirical conditions. As the statistics I cited in the previous
section indicate, the current global economic order is characterised by
profound poverty and inequality. What is more, the gulf between the global
haves and have-nots has significantly increased over the past fifteen years.
Thus, the demise of ostensive economic alternatives to capitalism coincides
with an increase in poverty and inequality. Finally, no one could possibly
dispute the dominance of the affluent societies within the regulatory global
financial institutions. One may, for the time being, set aside the question
why delegates and representatives act in the way they do in these fora, whilst
accepting that the consequences of these actions are, generally, detrimental
to those whose lack of political influence mirrors their economic vulnerability. One need not, therefore, accept all of Pogge's claims in drawing the
conclusion that the predominant form which global capitalism presently
takes coincides with gross economic inequalities, and that the consequences
of these conditions are devastating for many. It may not always and forever

be the case that capitalism creates and exacerbates inequality. What is clear is that this is very much the case today.

The second category of obstacle to overcoming global inequality consists of a variety of different international institutions the basis and general functioning of which serve to obstruct an effective remedy to the problem. I shall begin with an analysis of the United Nations and its approach towards economic, social and cultural rights.

There has long been a view that economic, social and cultural rights are typically considered to be of less importance than their civil and political counterparts within the UN system (Hunt, 1996). I argued in an earlier chapter that the UN's ability to protect and promote human rights is significantly constrained by the organisation's structure and, in particular, the ability of member states to assert their national sovereignty over and against UN attempts to promote human rights. It would be fair to say that these restrictions apply even more forcefully to the attempt to establish and uphold commitments to overcoming global inequality. There are a number of relevant factors in this regard. Thus, the benchmark for establishing civil and political rights is typically seen as being far more clear-cut than for economic and social rights, which have a more inherently progressive dimension to them. States use this lack of specificity to justify their lack of progress in overcoming absolute poverty in their midst. This is further compounded by enduring disputes concerning the justiciable status of economic, social and cultural rights commitments. Put simply, legal redress and the prospect of legal consequences have been far more prominent and relatively more effective for civil and political rights. The argument is that identifying a violation of an individual's right to vote is so much more determinable and less disputable than identifying a violation of an individual's right to adequate housing, for example (Cranston, 1973). This particular argument has been presented by both affluent and poor member states in their response to criticism that not enough is being done to uphold economic, social and cultural rights commitments.

Similarly, many poor states have also resorted to the, on the face of it not unreasonable, argument that they simply lack the resources to eradicate poverty by themselves and require greater international assistance and aid to do so. To this extent, their calls for help have received only a modest response. Very few affluent states come close to meeting the UN stipulated minimum of 0.7 per cent of GDP in overseas development aid (ODA). To make matters even worse, much ODA takes the form of financial and technical support the express aim of which is to produce the goods and markets required by affluent societies (George, 1988 and 1992). Very little, if any, ODA can be described as genuinely 'altruistic' in the true sense of the word. A significant proportion of this aid has failed to meet even the relatively modest targets set by the donors.

One may, initially at least, counter-pose this critical account of the UN with the example of its commitment towards the so-called Millennium goals. The Millennium goals emerged out of theWorld Food Summit in Rome, 1996. This gathering was organised by the UN's Food and Agriculture Organisation (FAO). All of the participating member states agreed to 'pledge our political will and our common and national commitment to achieving food security for all and to an on-going effort to eradicate hunger in all countries, with an immediate view to reducing the number of undernourished people to half their present level no later than 2015' (1996, cited in Pogge, 2002: 10). The Millennium goals extend beyond a mere concern for food security and eradicating malnutrition to encompass aspirations to overcome a wider set of poverty-related conditions. As such, they represent a noble gesture and express the manifest aspirations of the international community. However, progress towards realising these goals has been slow and fitful. Recently, the former UN Secretary-General, Kofi Annan, admitted that few, if any, of the Millennium goals will be successfully attained by 2015 (BBC, April 2008). Thomas Pogge (2002) predicts that current global economic trends suggest that the poor will be even poorer in 2015 than they were in 2000. This prediction predates the economic crises of 2008 and the likely consequences of these upon affluent countries' willingness to promote the economic interests of others.

The other principal institutional obstacle to overcoming global inequalities is the World Trade Organisation (WTO). The WTO replaced its predecessor, GATT, in 1995. Its principal function and remit are to promote and regulate free trade. It comprises over 180 member nation-states. As it stands, the WTO is clearly more important for global trade as a specific phenomenon than the UN. Indeed, the UN's ability to promote and protect economic, social and cultural rights is obviously profoundly affected by the policies and decisions of the WTO. The WTO has attracted a great deal of criticism over recent years (Bhagwati, 2000). Quite apart from its stated purpose of promoting the conditions for fair trade, much of the academic criticism has focused upon the WTO's structure and management. In effect, the organisation has been frequently criticised for promoting the economic interests of its most powerful members. If these interests are consistent with the removal of tariffs and expensive regulations then free trade policies typically ensue. However, in certain circumstances, the removal of tariffs and import quotas, in particular, have been opposed by the more powerful members as contrary to their economic interests. The consequence of this has been to make it more difficult for developing-world producers to sell and export their produce into the more affluent markets (Pogge, 2002). The WTO may therefore be criticised for ultimately succumbing to political interests and pressure. For Pogge the organisation exists not to promote global free trade, but to maintain and strengthen the economic hegemony of the powerful at the expense of the powerless. Causality is a difficult attribute fully to identify and substantiate. Whether or not the WTO ultimately and directly exacerbates global inequality is a moot point. What can be unequivocally demonstrated, however, is that during the period of the WTO's existence global economic inequality has worsened. It may not, necessarily, be the cause of the problem but, so far at least, it clearly has not proved to be a remedy.

The first two factors might be thought of as external factors; they emanate outside poor regions and are beyond the control of those the populations of which are most afflicted by the effects of global inequality. The third factor consists of internal elements and conditions. In particular, we need to single out indigenous infrastructure and political corruption as two important contributors to the plight of the impoverished. In referring to these factors as internal conditions one should be mindful of the danger of simply blaming the poor for their own plight, as some have undoubtedly done. Lack of infrastructure and political corruption impact upon the poor, but they have often had little opportunity to exercise any influence upon or control over these conditions. While lack of infrastructure may result in or be affected by the geographical and environmental composition of particular environments, political corruption is typically associated with the absence of effective democratic institutions and practices. It is clearly counter-intuitive to assume that, given the choice, the poor would actively affirm such conditions. Nevertheless they are relevant and cannot be so directly laid at the door of powerful and wealthy nations.

As I stated earlier in this chapter, the last decade has witnessed a shift away from a focus upon aid towards trade as the principal means by which the poor can overcome their economic plight. Generally, this has involved attempts to develop closer trading relationships between poor producers and affluent consumers. This has not proceeded as smoothly as many would have hoped. Part of the reason for this is the continuing existence of import tariffs and quotas which trading blocs such as the United States and the European Union have insisted upon maintaining. However, trade and not aid has clearly been established as the principal means for overcoming global poverty. One obvious obstacle to securing these exchange relationships concerns infrastructure. Producers need to get their goods from where they are grown to airports or ports. This requires reliable roads and transport links. The lack of such fundamental infrastructural conditions can have a devastating effect upon such markets. Needless to say, the development of reliable and effective transport infrastructure is comparatively expensive and typically falls upon governments and public authorities to finance. The poorer a country is, the more difficult it will be to pay for such infrastructural developments, and so the less revenue it will be able to raise through taxing the production of cash crops. An exclusive focus upon trade at the expense of aid will most likely trap the poorest countries and regions in a vicious circle of underdevelopment. Addressing this problem will require the provision of overseas development aid, and thus the economic support of the affluent countries of the world.

Arguably an even more protracted problem concerns internal political corruption. Political corruption is another internal factor which plays an important role in exacerbating existing poverty in poor, particularly authoritarian countries. Put simply, the wealth which does flow into a country or a region is diverted into the accounts of a corrupt political élite. Political corruption exists everywhere and to varying degrees. However, its prevalence in some parts of the world has devastating consequences for the poorest sections of those populations. Africa is conventionally considered to be most affected by political corruption, with present-day Zimbabwe providing a good example. However, other regions of the world are also significantly affected. Myanmar (Burma) for example is a country which continues to export significant quantities of crude oil whilst much of its population languishes in absolute poverty. The lack of effective democratic institutions and ensuing authoritarian rule facilitates corrupt élites' accumulation of vast personal fortunes based upon the plundering of their countries' wealth and economic resources. This accumulation of private fortunes serves further to impoverish their populations whilst allowing the extension and consolidation of their own power, which, in turn, has made it even more difficult for these populations to challenge this monopolisation of power. It is a truly vicious circle. It is valid, I believe, to characterise infrastructural underdevelopment and political corruption as internal factors. However, as I mentioned above, this does not mean that we may somehow blame the poor for their own plight. Overcoming such obstacles will require significant external support and assistance. This will need to take different forms, including affluent countries' governments placing far more effective pressure upon corrupt political élites. It will also require the provision of targeted aid to ensure the development of an infrastructure which is fit for the task of developing and extending complex exchange relationships. While these appear necessary, realising such proposals will have to overcome the very real problem that the persistence of these conditions may be perceived as serving the ostensive economic and political interests of the affluent and the powerful. The developed world's dependence upon crude oil, for example, is a fundamental factor in determining foreign policy in parts of the world where human rights are routinely abused but upon which we may be dependent for our energy supplies. Confronting this perception and calculation of interests requires an appeal to morality, which leads us to the final obstacle in overcoming global economic inequality.

I stated earlier that we may assume that the effects of global poverty (as exemplified by the morbidity and mortality data I presented) will appear morally unacceptable to many. Few people would positively affirm starvation and poverty as a morally neutral concern. Some people are even compelled to donate to charity or protest to politicians in the face of global poverty. However, the fact is that the vast majority of affluent populations take no concerted action to support their moral belief that global poverty is wrong. On the face of it, we would have to say that global poverty is largely ignored by those not afflicted by its effects. In respect of this particular area of moral concern, belief and consequent action are at odds with one another.

Thomas Pogge devotes a significant part of his analysis of human rights and poverty to the role of affluent consumers' contribution to the persistence of global poverty. He adopts, it is fair to say, an unequivocal position on the issue. He states: 'extensive, severe poverty can continue, because we do not find its eradication morally compelling' (2002: 3). He acknowledges that there are exceptions to this particular rule and that their positive effects should not be dismissed. However, the fact that they are exceptional demonstrates the basic contradiction between what many affluent consumers and citizens morally believe and what they are prepared to do. This dissonance between belief and action should not be thought of as a mere lapse in logic or reason. Pogge argues that part of the motive for doing nothing consists in the economic benefits which accrue to many in the developed world. Put simply, our own material welfare benefits from the economic impoverishment of others. The deflated prices of cash crops and the relatively cheap prices for many manufactured goods are dependent upon low wages, 'liberal' employment conditions and regulations, and strict controls on commodity prices. We are wealthier as a consequence of our counterparts' poverty. Many of us will lament the suffering of others but few, it seems, are prepared to forego any benefits or incur any costs in support of our somewhat 'cheap' moral commitments. This discrepancy between belief and action on the part of those of us who benefit economically from the persistence of global inequality presents an important obstacle to overcoming global inequality.

As with all of the above factors considered in this section, the issue of an apparent conflict between moral beliefs and subsequent action is complex. Pogge's morally unequivocal stance draws upon an overtly emotivist characterisation of moral judgement. In so doing it fails to address important questions. For example, his position assumes that moral interests and economic interests can cohere. This is a significant assumption. We must ask whether the fact that affluent consumers do appear to economically benefit from others' poverty can simply be set aside in an insistence that this stop. Similarly, Pogge's position rests upon an assumption that the establishment of a single economic space entails the acceptance of a corresponding and single moral space or community. One may identify affluent consumers' actions as an important element in maintaining global inequality. One may just as incontrovertibly identify a clear

discrepancy between many consumers' moral beliefs regarding global inequality and their subsequent willingness to alter their behaviour. To this extent,
these are important contributory factors in maintaining global inequality.
Alongside the dominance of capitalism, the role of international institutions
and the prevalence of underdeveloped infrastructure and political corruption,
these constitute fundamental elements in maintaining the current global
economic order.

Having established the scale of the problem of global inequality and
presented some of the key obstacles to overcoming the symptoms of the
phenomenon, the discussion must now turn towards a consideration of what
can be done to confront and begin to alleviate the suffering of others in this
respect.

DUTY AND GLOBAL INEQUALITY

The aim of this chapter is to confront a view of human rights which holds that
the possession of rights requires little positive action or commitment on the
part of others. I am arguing that this particular view amounts to a significant
misunderstanding of human rights to the extent that it neglects the indispensable importance of the establishment and maintenance of distinct social, political and economic frameworks within which rights may be possessed and,
more importantly, exercised. This final and longest section of this chapter
presents an argument in defence of the necessity of consolidating and enforc-
ing duties as a means of responding to global inequality. This might be thought
of by some as a particularly difficult or ambitious test case for the defence of
the importance of correlative duties as counterparts to the promotion and
protection of fundamental human rights to a secure material existence. So be
it. If my argument proves persuasive then we may extend its claims to the
remainder of the human rights doctrine. If it does not, then my failure will not
thereby serve to condemn the argument in favour of recognising the need for
duty *per se*, but only of seeking to extend it this far. Rather than delve straight
into the arguments in favour of my position, I shall begin by discussing those
who are overtly opposed to both the letter and the spirit of my claims.

Reduced to its bare essentials this issue concerns the question whether or
not there exists a duty to alleviate the suffering of the globally impoverished.
Phrased in this way, there may appear to be only one conceivably legitimate
answer. However, we have already seen that the ostensibly morally imperative
character of one's evaluation of global inequality rapidly begins to dissolve
when one seeks to carry the principle through to action and policy. This
suggests that the situation may be rather more complex than many might
initially imagine. Boldly stated, the principle of a moral duty to alleviate

global poverty is far too general and abstract to provide answers to important questions. Thus, we must ask who ought to help and who ought to be helped. In addition and just as importantly, we need to know what form this help should take. Questions such as these primarily concern the appropriate means for realising what is assumed to be a valid end. Not everyone, however, accepts this principle. Some have consistently challenged the claim that there exists a moral duty to help to alleviate global poverty, or that any such duty could be justifiably established.

Placed in its most general context, the academic debate between those who support the principle and those who oppose it can be cast in a framework which distinguishes between cosmopolitan theorists in support of it and nationalists and realists who oppose it. I will consider the supporters' position in due course. However, I begin by examining the arguments presented by the opponents to the principle. I start by discussing the so-called 'nationalist' argument presented by David Miller (1995 and 2000) and then proceed to consider the realist arguments outlined by the likes of George Keenan (1964) and Kenneth Waltz.

The most consistent and detailed case in support of a nationalist approach to the issue of global poverty and moral responsibilities towards others has been presented by the political theorist David Miller. The core of his argument is a claim that the primary entity in global political relations is the nation-state. The nation-state is the political roof under which citizens with a shared national identity live and principally relate to one another. Miller rejects the counterpart view presented by defenders of ethical cosmopolitanism which holds that there exists an underlying single and global moral community. For Miller, this vision of a single global community is a mere figment of some people's imagination and has no established basis in contemporary political reality. For the basis of rejecting the existence of a single and global moral community, Miller proceeds to argue that citizens' legal responsibilities and duties extend no further than to members of the same political communities: if we owe duties to any other individuals, these extend to include only other members of the same nation-state. Miller (2000) underlines this argument with an explicit rejection of the claim that the affluent are under a moral duty to assist the suffering of the poor in other parts of the world. He insists, however, that he is not to be thereby understood as endorsing a position such as that found within Robert Nozick's work, which opposes all forms of redistributive assistance and taxation. Miller accepts that some degree of wealth redistribution occurs in most, if not all, developed and affluent nation-states and finds no general fault with such welfare systems. Indeed, Miller conceives of the legitimacy of welfare states as based upon their function as schemes of mutual and reciprocal assistance. These systems can work and are legitimate only to the extent that they are limited to members of the same nation-state: the same basic community. Extending their application beyond these parameters serves to undermine citizens' willingness to contribute to these schemes through, amongst other things, their likely inability to identify and empathise with these 'outsiders'. Thus, Miller argues that cosmopolitanism is confronted by and cannot overcome a basic feature of human psychology: our motivation to help others diminishes the further away from us (literally and figuratively) these others are. He bolsters this argument with a further claim that very few, if any, individual citizens think of themselves as members of a single global moral community. Instead, he insists, we tend to think of ourselves as belonging to distinct and bounded communities. We may accept a moral duty to assist other members of the same community, but we tend not to extend this concern beyond the borders of our own community. We are less cosmopolitans and more nationalists in respect of our moral consideration for the welfare of others. This, then, is a claim about human psychology and motivational structures.

Miller also argues that each nation-state has the principal duty to assist its own citizens. With the notable exception of stateless persons, we are all citizens of at least one nation-state, whichever it may be. Miller insists that the extent of our claims upon others to assist is set by our citizenship status. Each of our respective states has a moral duty to help us, its individual citizens, when help is required. He accepts that many states systematically fail adequately to discharge and uphold this duty. However, responsibility for this lies with the state in question. He insists that simply because some states fail in this regard does not provide an argument for the claim that the responsibility must then shift to other states or bodies of citizens.

As our example of a nationalist position on the question of the basis and scope of a duty to assist others, Miller's argument comprises two distinct elements: a claim about the basis and reach of identity as a criterion for the willingness to assist others and an appeal to the state-centric structure of the global political infrastructure. On the face of it, Miller might appear to base his argument on relatively hard and uncontroversial empirical truths: not everyone will normatively approve of such truths, but the truths remain nevertheless. Thus, it is legally accurate to say that nation-states have the primary duty of care towards their own citizens. Similarly, it simply is the case that the vast majority of people take little or no effective action to assist others and that the willingness to do so diminishes the further away these others are. We might, therefore, say that these aspects of Miller's position possess some descriptive force. However, this conclusion does not settle the issue. We need to ask whether the apparently descriptive force of his claims is sufficient for substantiating the normative claims he presents. Following on from this, we must also ask whether these descriptions themselves can be challenged or alternatively interpreted. I shall consider these questions in reverse order.

A number of theorists have argued that the nation-state is not as central and significant to the geo-political order as was once the case (Caney, 2005; Held, 2006; Scheffler, 2001). Caney supports this claim, in part, by means of a specific analysis of Miller's argument. Caney argues, in effect, that the nation-state was a distinct historical and political creation, the status and features of which have altered over time and across regions. On this view, Miller may be criticised for attempting to de-historicise and essentialise the nation-state. Because he operates with an unduly de-historicised and essentialised notion of the nation-state, Miller appears to overlook or ignore the effects of globalising forces upon the capacity of any state fully to protect its borders, so to speak. Thus, Caney argues that Miller presents a false description and interpretation of the nation-state in the contemporary age. Caney also insists that advocates of nationalism in this context obscure from view empirical phenomena which challenge the nationalist picture: for example, the existence of wider regional and global networks through which communities of people come together despite their national differences. Miller is thereby criticised for misrepresenting the status and contemporary function of the nation-state.

Caney also challenges Miller on normative grounds. Thus, Caney argues that even if Miller's purported descriptions of the contemporary nation-state and the corresponding geo-political order were accurate, merely pointing to how things are (or at least how things appear to be) does not suffice to support a correlative normative claim. Facts do not validate norms. If this were the case, the human rights project would never have got off the ground. Nor would any other emancipatory project the very *raison d'être* of which was the precise denial of the factual, empirical conditions these projects aimed at creating. One ought to be able to analyse the structure of Miller's nationalist argument in these terms, regardless of whether one normatively supports or opposes the position in question. The nationalist position exemplified by Miller is thereby criticised for being unduly partial. The account rests upon a limited and somewhat anachronistic assumption that the nation-state remains a largely autonomous and effectively sovereign entity and a similarly partial normative conclusion that the purportedly empirical hegemony of the nation-state is itself morally desirable. Ironically perhaps, nationalism may thereby be condemned for resting its claims upon an unsubstantiated premise which is not sufficiently supported by contemporary geo-political realities. Nation-states and their populations actually co-exist within a political, economic and technological framework which dissolves and diminishes the importance of national frontiers. Nationalism may be criticised for ignoring, or failing to pay due attention to, the fact of globalisation. However, nationalism does not exhaust the stock of arguments presented against the legitimacy of a duty to assist others in upholding their fundamental human rights. The other principal opponent consists of realism.

Akin to its nationalist counterpart, the realist position is based upon a rejection of cosmopolitanism as utopian and unworkable. Realists argue that one may imagine and conceive of principles which ground a duty to assist others beyond the frontiers of one's own political communities, but that all such projects will inevitably run aground on the realities of global geo-politics. The realist position includes a number of specific claims and arguments. Thus, Kenneth Waltz (1979) proposes the so-called 'systemic argument', which insists that individual states cannot, in fact, act in the manner and to the extent that a duty to assist distant others would require. Waltz insists that the global system does not allow states to do anything other than pursue and promote their own separate and partial interests. Global politics is a game played by states in accordance with relatively strict rules and conventions. These rules and conventions effectively restrict any single state's capacity to pursue altruism at the expense of self-interested objectives. States which do not assert and pursue their own interests will themselves suffer as a consequence.

George Keenan (1964) presents a further argument against the existence of cosmopolitan duties. Keenan draws upon the contractarian tradition of liberal political theory when he writes that states have a fundamental and contractual duty to their own citizens first and foremost. Hypothetically at least, states are formed and maintained through communities of individuals entering into a political contract with one another as a means to promote and pursue individual self-interest. The legitimacy of the state is dependent upon its willingness and ability to maintain the conditions which enable this pursuit of self-interest to occur peacefully and effectively. One specific way in which the state discharges its duty towards its own citizens is in the restriction of access to its resources. Put simply, Keenan argues that states have a moral duty to assist their own citizens first and foremost. Diverting resources to helping and assisting citizens of other nation-states is condemned as a diminution or violation of this duty. On this view, each state's moral duty to assist begins and ends very firmly 'at home'.

Realism has, like its nationalist counterpart, been subjected to extensive criticism (Barry, 1991; Beitz, 1999; Caney, 2005). Indeed, realism falls foul of very similar problems and limitations to those which afflict nationalism. Generally, one may say that both Waltz and Keenan base their position upon a similarly partial and limited description of how the world actually is. Thus, Waltz's argument is fundamentally based upon the claim that individual nation-states are involved in a competitive game, the assumption being that this game is being played on a relatively level playing field. This claim is manifestly false. In the real world, individual nation-states have vastly differing stocks of resources, power, capital and influence. This disparity means that some states do, in fact, have sufficient resources to help others without undermining or adversely affecting their fundamental interests. A second ground upon which realism may be criticised counters the claim that individual nation-states *per se* are best placed to assist their own citizens. If this is a mere issue of resources then it is manifestly false. Many of the poorer states in the world do not possess sufficient resources for adequately securing the basic economic and social rights of their own citizens. This is a simple fact. This, after all, provides the very basis for programmes of international assistance. Realists can be accused of operating with an undue (arguably unrealistic) account of the nation-state. In an international context, what is most important about nation-states is not their formal similarities, but rather their substantive differences. When one combines these two criticisms realism begins to resemble an attempt to justify existing inequalities and power imbalances. The normative thrust of realism consists of an attempt to affirm the current global order which offers justification for the most powerful to continue organising the world in ways which appear to enhance their ostensive interests in an unequal and unjust global order.

Both nationalism and realism may be criticised on the basis of their respective empirical claims and, perhaps slightly more tentatively at this point, the moral impoverishment of their normative claims. The contemporary global order is very much more interconnected than either nationalists or realists seem willing fully to accept. Generally, this interconnectedness continues to expose the poorer and less powerful populations of the world to an order which ostensibly benefits their affluent and powerful counterparts. The facts which continue to matter and are most demanding of our concern are those cited earlier in this chapter which continue to testify to the awful consequences of present global realities. What have been established so far are the weaknesses and limitations of the opponents' positions and arguments. As such, these weaknesses and limitations do not suffice to validate the claim in support of a duty to help the poor. While the morbidity and mortality data of global inequality testify to the moral urgency of addressing these conditions, they cannot provide a sufficiently detailed formulation and justification for what must be done.

The intellectual basis and context for developing a response to global poverty is cosmopolitanism and its insistence that all human beings, ultimately, inhabit a single and global moral community. In addition to cosmopolitanism's account of the basis of our membership of a single moral community, the doctrine also holds that the moral claims and status of each human being are not conditional upon his or her geographical location or social affiliation. All human beings have an equal moral claim to be free from the effects or threat of systematic and significant suffering. The extent to which this is manifestly not the case provides a fundamental element of cosmopolitanism's critique of existing global realities. While national frontiers are clearly less effective and formidable than they once might have been,

exposure to the conditions which my account of human rights aims to overcome remains largely a consequence of geographical location, compounded by
subsequent internal political oppression and the abuse of power. An effective
response to the effects of global poverty must begin with a context which
encompasses all human beings, whilst recognising the extent to which a
minority of human beings are largely protected from the conditions of absolute
poverty which afflict the majority. As a means of establishing the moral basis
for an argument based upon an appeal to a duty to confront the effects of
global poverty, I shall consider three separate cosmopolitan analyses of the
phenomenon found in the work of Henry Shue (1996), Hillel Steiner (1994)
and Thomas Pogge (2002).

Shue bases his case for global economic justice upon his account of basic
needs. He insists that all human beings have an equal moral right to the means
of a basic subsistence; a right which countless millions of individuals are
being denied. Shue advocates a form of *rights holism*. That is to say, he insists
that human rights exist as an integrated package and cannot be rank-ordered in
terms of relative importance. Thus, for Shue economic and social rights are
necessary for all other rights. Put simply, if one lacks the basic means for
subsistence one is unable to enjoy the exercise of any right. Economic and
social rights are necessary means for all rights. For him, the effects of global
poverty are not restricted to economic and social rights but extend to affect all
rights adversely. Hunger, poverty and ill-health significantly undermine the
exercise of free speech, free assembly and all other civil and political rights.
Shue is a cosmopolitan to the extent that he insists that the case for global
economic justice is ultimately based upon the equal moral value and standing
of all human beings, irrespective of where they happen to have been born.

Hillel Steiner's argument draws more comprehensively upon an appeal to
the equality principle. Steiner views the equality principle as both being
central to any rights-based argument and requiring that all human beings have
a right to enjoy a broadly equal enjoyment of and access to the earth's natural
resources. According to Steiner, global inequality is primarily the result of the
wealthy exploiting the earth's natural resources and, in various ways, gaining
more than their fair share at the expense of the poor. Steiner's argument inten-
tionally disregards national frontiers. It also runs entirely counter to international property law, the purpose of which, for the most part, is to provide legal
validation for plundering the world's resources in a fashion which perpetuates
and deepens inequality.

Thomas Pogge provides a more detailed and comprehensive account of a
cosmopolitan global ethics than either Shue or Steiner. As I demonstrated
earlier in this chapter, Pogge presents an account of the causes of global
inequality which lays responsibility very clearly at the feet of those affluent
and powerful societies which would appear to gain the greatest material

advantage from regulating global markets in a manner which denies entire regions and societies access to the bare essentials of life. However, Pogge is not content simply to point the finger and condemn insofar as he proposes an initial programme of action for responding to, in the first instance at least, the effects of absolute poverty. Pogge argues that the problem lies in the distribution of global resources and that the beginnings of a solution must therefore be sought in a scheme of redistributing some resources from the affluent towards the poor. He proposes a scheme which, if implemented, he claims would eradicate absolute poverty and inject huge sums of money into the economies of the poor. He advocates a redistributive mechanism, which he calls the 'global resources dividend' (GRD). The GRD would consist of a $2 dividend on each barrel of crude oil produced throughout the world. This would add a largely insignificant amount to each litre of petrol but would raise a sum of money which would exceed the current overseas development aid of the wealthy countries by over six times, which, if fairly distributed, would enable the poor countries quickly to overcome and eradicate forms of absolute poverty among their populations.[1] Pogge insists that this is fundamentally fair insofar as it involves giving up some very small part of the wealth which was unfairly accumulated in the first place. The initial aim of Pogge's scheme would be to eradicate absolute poverty with the intention of developing far fairer rules and procedures for regulating global trade and economic exchange in due course.

Pogge's proposal would entail consumers bearing some small part of the burden of overcoming absolute poverty. Needless to say, his proposal remains merely that. However, the principle of consumers paying more for commodities in the name of economic justice has achieved some limited success in the phenomenon of fair trade. I argued in an earlier work (Fagan, 2006b) that fair trade offers relatively affluent consumers the opportunity of buying goods that have been certified as non-exploitative to the producers of those goods. Thus, for example, fair trade coffee typically costs more than its non-fair-trade counterpart. The additional cost comprises a guaranteed 'bonus' (somewhere between five and ten per cent of the market value of a kilo of coffee beans) which is paid directly to the producers of the crop. Many of these producers are organised into co-operatives and the additional price they receive for their produce is intended to be reinvested in local community projects and infrastructure. The same process and principle apply to a wide range of other goods and produce. Fair trade defies the conventional motive of consumers for maximising their own economic value. Fair trade consumers are prepared, it would appear at least, to put their money where their mouths are, to coin a

---

[1]   Readers may wish to compare this proposal with the so-called 'Tobin tax'. See Patomaki, 2001.

phrase. Fair trade has been criticised (*Economist*, December 2006) on various grounds. Conventional advocates of free-market trade view the phenomenon as a distortion of the market. Placing these concerns to one side, market share of fair-trade goods is fractional, consisting of 0.01 per cent of global trade in 2004 (Fagan, 2006b). This indicates a clear potential for growth but also demonstrates the limited potential of fair trade to overcome or significantly alleviate the effects of global poverty. Shopping, by itself, is not going to solve the problem.

On the face of it, initiatives like fair trade and proposals such as Pogge's represent hard-headed attempts to think and act through a response to global poverty. In general terms, they are both worthy of further support. However, neither of them fully engages with the issue of a potential duty to seek to alleviate the suffering caused by global poverty. Pogge discusses the notion of duty but does not fully integrate this into his precise proposal. Advocates of fair trade tend to market the phenomenon as a morally good thing to do, but do not typically go so far as to argue that consumers should be duty-bound to opt for fair-trade goods. The act of buying fair trade products appears, if not discretionary, then at least what moral philosophers term supererogatory: morally valuable acts above and beyond the reasonable demands of duty (Bradley, 1999). In this way, those who seek to take some action against global poverty are likely to be characterised as 'moral saints' (Wolf, 1982). What is lost from this view is the notion of duty, which I shall now attempt to reinsert into the debate over what should be done in the face of global poverty.

As I stated at the beginning of this chapter, human rights have been criticised by some for allegedly ignoring or even undermining the importance of duty as a moral good. On this view, human rights are viewed as promoting individually selfish desires which, by appeal to the language of rights, seek to transform mere wants into apparent needs. Human rights are accused of inflating individuals' demands upon the state and others. The discussion of Chapter 1 addressed this particular phenomenon and acknowledged the threat it poses to the continuing legitimacy of the doctrine. However, a proper and sufficiently comprehensive understanding of human rights must extend to include the necessity of duty as a correlate of any and all human rights (Jones, 1994). Rights necessarily correlate with duties. Both must be seen as attributes and components of a specific approach to regulating human relations with a distinct social, political and economic framework. Human rights exist not because individual human beings are radically separate from one another but, on the contrary, because of the degree to which we are exposed to one another and, to some extent and in some respects, mutually dependent upon one another. A one-dimensional focus upon rights, at the expense of duties, ignores what we might term the inherent sociality of human rights. Human rights may well have become a tool for some whose motives are primarily selfish, but the account of human rights which underlies any and all such uses is fundamentally false as a consequence of its partiality and neglect for duty.

The concept of duty has long been the object of philosophical concern from the earliest to the most recent days of the discipline. When applied to the specific institution of human rights a number of questions demand satisfactory answers. The first concerns why duty can be defended as indispensable to the possession of rights. I have alluded to the broad outline of an answer to this question above, but will return to it in a moment. The second concerns who possesses human rights-based duties and to whom are these duties owed. Finally, we must address the issue of how these duties may be discharged and what form they ought to take. I will consider each in turn before concluding Chapter 6.

Joel Feinberg (1980) and Peter Jones (1994) both defend what has become referred to as the 'correlativity thesis', which holds that rights necessarily correlate with duties. These may take either negative or positive forms. Thus, my right to life imposes a negative duty upon others not to interfere with or seek to infringe that right. It also extends to the imposition of positive duties upon others, primarily the state, to provide for that right in the form of sufficient security and access to health-care if and when I require it. My right to life would amount to a purely and entirely abstract entity in the absence of the corresponding and correlative duties. As I argued above, this underlines what is often overlooked in discussions about the basis of human rights: that they are inherently and necessarily socially based and constituted forms. Human rights might, conceivably at least, still exist in the absence of duty, but their existence would be merely rhetorical and their capacity to effect change practically impotent. In my opinion, none of these claims are particularly controversial. Nor does the existence of duty *per se* provide the real source of dispute and debate in this particular area. What is really in question is not so much whether rights correlate with duties, but rather what the implications of this relationship may be. When applied to global poverty, the fundamental questions revolve around concerns over the scope of duties to help others and upon whom such duties legitimately fall. Put bluntly, how burdensome will such duties prove to be?

In accepting the uncontroversial claim that rights correlate with duties, one is bound to accept that the possession and exercise of economic, social and cultural rights are dependent upon the establishment and maintenance of corresponding duties. This will require the establishment of a material framework of regulated institutions and relations which are necessary for protecting and promoting these fundamental human rights. The existence of absolute poverty constitutes a fundamental obstacle to realising this end. While relative poverty is an inherent feature of all systems of economic wealth and exchange, the prevalence of absolute poverty is largely restricted to specific regions of the world and is, to this extent, localised. Establishing an admittedly rather crude distinction between the 'haves' and the 'have-nots' is therefore a relatively uncomplicated task. Based on the premise that the burden of duty falls upon those with the resources and means to discharge the duties concerned, we may argue that the duty to protect and promote, in the first instance, the economic, social and cultural rights of the absolutely poor ought to fall upon the affluent parts of the world. While the state remains a principal agent in the global political order, the scope of human rights principles is not restricted by national frontiers. If a particular state is unwilling or unable to uphold its human rights commitments to its own population, then human rights advocates are entitled to look beyond this context in the search to identify those who do have the requisite resources in this respect.

As we saw above, not everyone accepts the basis and terms of an argument in support of cosmopolitan duties towards others. Nationalists and realists both, in their respective ways, oppose any such account. However, both positions are significantly flawed and leave intact a global situation which condemns millions to misery and premature death. Others have accepted the necessity of responding to global poverty by appeal to the legitimacy of cosmopolitan duties. These include philosophers such as Brian Barry (1991) and Charles Beitz (1999). Both argue for the existence of a duty to assist others to overcome the suffering caused by absolute poverty. Both also argue that this duty falls primarily upon the affluent sections of the globe. However, they differ in respect of whom each identifies as the duty-bearer in this regard. Thus, Brian Barry argues that affluent states, individually and collectively, are the most effective and thus legitimate duty-bearers. Affluent states possess the greatest resources and power, and provide the most effective source for alleviating the effects of global suffering through increasing such existing mechanisms as overseas development aid and pursuing a global regulatory economic system which promotes the capacity of the poor to trade their way out of absolute poverty. In contrast, Charles Beitz argues that the duty falls primarily not upon states, but upon individuals. Beitz argues that individuals in the affluent parts of the world have a moral duty to assist their counterparts in the poor parts of the world. He derives this duty by appeal to the existence of a global moral community consisting of all individual human beings possessing broadly equal moral status and standing. Beitz argues that global poverty has not been effectively responded to, in part because individuals living in the affluent regions of the world have all too often simply delegated their responsibility towards others to their respective states. Affluent states have proven to be largely ineffective in alleviating the problem for a variety of complex reasons. Beitz insists that the failure of states obscures individual responsibility. Individuals, he argues, have a moral duty both to refrain from systematically behaving in ways which manifestly harm the absolute poor and actively to work towards overcoming the suffering of others through individual actions and commitments. Examples of this might include buying fair-trade goods, donating time and money to appropriate organisations, and pressuring elected representatives to direct state resources to this end. For Beitz, individual action and inaction contribute significantly and directly to the suffering of others whom we are separated from only by morally irrelevant frontiers.

The final issue concerns what form, or 'currency', any such duty-bound assistance should take. This is not as straightforward as some might initially imagine. The conventional response is likely to focus upon monetary goods, such as credit transfers, the cancelling of debt repayments, and the financing of various projects. On this view, the affluent might better discharge their duties by greater expenditure of monetary wealth. The measure of the effect of such an approach is then most likely to consist of calculations of increases in gross domestic product (GDP) and calculations of the overall levels of wealth in a particular country or region in receipt of such financial assistance. However, others have sought to challenge or revise this approach. Thus, the Nobel laureate Amartya Sen (1999b) has argued that financial capital is not the most effective means of raising living standards and securing basic human rights.

Sen has presented an intricate and very detailed analysis of economic development. He argues that the World Bank's traditional focus upon GDP as a measure of a country's wealth is of limited value. It does not demonstrate how that wealth is distributed within a particular country, and thus does not provide a sufficiently reliable indicator for determining the spread of wealth within a population. Countries with relatively high GDPs may nevertheless contain extensive populations of absolutely impoverished people, while countries with modest GDPs may nevertheless distribute that wealth in a more equitable manner, so that no one is exposed to conditions of absolute poverty. Like John Rawls (1971) before him, Sen insists that economic justice must be measured by appeal to the conditions of the least well-off in any given country. Sen also proceeds to challenge the focus upon monetary wealth as the sole currency of assistance. While economic spending power is obviously not to be underestimated, Sen argues that development should ultimately be measured by reference to what he refers to as people's 'basic capabilities' to develop and pursue their own projects and life-plans. At root, these will include such 'goods' as access to clean drinking water, adequate shelter, the means for enjoying a sustainable and adequate diet, access to educational resources and the like. Many, if not all, of these need to be paid for of course, but Sen insists that the ultimate form which development assistance should take should comprise institutions and resources which are fundamentally necessary for individual agency. On this view, money may be a means to an end but not be considered as an end in itself. The duties of the affluent towards the poor should, therefore, take the form of the transfer of wealth and the promotion of resources for overcoming absolute poverty in pursuit of an expanding capacity for agency.

CONCLUSION

I have argued that global inequality and the sheer extent of absolute poverty constitute the gravest and most systematic human rights abuse in the contemporary world. The causes of this ongoing catastrophe are not natural or God-given, but result from the creation and maintenance of specific social, political and economic institutions. I have also argued that human rights correlate with duties. This contradicts an approach to human rights which condemns the doctrine as a mere mechanism for supporting and perpetuating selfish individualism. For human rights to be adequately protected there must exist institutions, agents and mechanisms which provide for their possession and exercise. This requires the establishment of clear and distinct duties. Global poverty indicates the extent to which the duties which correlate with economic, social and cultural rights are denied and ignored. The means for confronting, in the first instance, absolute poverty lie, in part, in the reassertion of duties to alleviate the suffering which results from absolute poverty. While it may be morally convenient to imagine otherwise, the onus for upholding the relevant duties does not fall exclusively upon states. As relatively affluent individuals there are many things we do which adversely impact upon the lives of others. Relatively insignificant and inexpensive alterations in our spending habits, for example, will have disproportionately beneficial effects upon the distant producers of the goods we consume. However, affluent states also have to bear a very great deal of responsibility for the suffering of others. While billions of dollars have been expended on ill-judged military campaigns, some of the most powerful and affluent nations have done very little to address global poverty. Indeed, in many instances such states have appeared to pursue policies which will serve only to compound and exacerbate the problem. Ultimately, the actions and policies of affluent and powerful states concern the electorates of those countries, and so the onus falls back upon individuals. The persistence of global poverty confronts the human rights project with a deep and formidable challenge. In conditions of global inequality, human rights for all are dependent upon the willingness of some to take a greater degree of responsibility for the suffering of others through the acceptance of those duties upon which the very infrastructure of human rights depends.

7. Accentuating the positive

INTRODUCTION

We have now reached the final chapter of this work. The previous chapters each addressed a particular myth or misunderstanding of human rights. While myths are characteristically more purposeful than misunderstandings, I have argued that the persistence of both is both potentially and actually harmful to the human rights cause. In contrast to those who have declared us to be living amidst a veritable age of human rights, I have argued that the status and possession of human rights are rather more tenuous and precarious than such pronouncements would suggest. In actual fact, human rights are abused everywhere. Some forms of abuse are long-standing and systematic, while others are more piecemeal and episodic. Human rights offer the vision of a world in which all human beings are free from the threat of systematic and significant suffering. Realising that vision remains a distant prospect for far too many and a constant reminder of how much human rights work remains to be done.

My analysis and discussion in the previous chapters have been, admittedly, somewhat negative in character. I have sought to find fault and weaknesses in other people's arguments and conceptions. Contrary to popular parlance (and having worked in both industries) the demolition of a structure actually is not any less difficult than the building of one. Each has its own particular set of specialised tasks and considerations. Each must be performed with care and attention. However, there is always something slightly disappointing about human endeavour which leaves nothing intact or standing. Readers typically expect (and may even be entitled to) the author's own alternative vision of that which he or she has carefully dismantled or undermined. A careful reading of the previous chapters is likely to reveal an immanent layer of argument and vision contained within my discussion. This chapter makes explicit what I consider to be the positive implications of the previously critical analysis. This is not intended to reinvent the wheel of human rights theory. In my opinion this is neither required nor feasible at the current time. It is, however, intended to leave the reader with a sufficiently clear account and understanding of how I conceive of the basis and limits of human rights as a moral and political doctrine. It also, of course, thereby provides an object for others' critical attention and analysis. The story thereby continues.

A MINIMALLY GOOD LIFE AS THE PREVENTION OF SYSTEMATIC SUFFERING

I argued in Chapter 1 for the need to avoid confusing human rights claims with other accounts and perspectives upon what it might be good for some to have access to and enjoy the exercise of. The discourse of human rights has travelled far beyond the confines of global institutions and the armchairs of academics. Many people across the globe have come to characterise their grievances and complaints in human rights terms. Broadly speaking the human rights community has good reasons to support and encourage this development. Extending the message of human rights can only strengthen the doctrine's appeal and moral authority. However, the diffusion of the message and appeal of human rights contains within it a particular challenge. At the core of this challenge stands a particular conception of human rights as a moral doctrine which encompasses an extensive and comprehensive range of human practices, beliefs, goods and wants. I argued that human rights have come to be seen by too many as a fully comprehensive moral doctrine, or what political and moral philosophers are wont to call a comprehensive conception of the good. Ostensibly there are clear reasons why such a mythical view should have developed. Human rights are, after all, typically concerned with matters of life and death. The international legal framework of human rights also encompasses a very wide-ranging collection of instruments designed to protect and promote a wide range of human goods, from a right to life and to be free from torture to rights to enjoy paid holidays from work. Human rights' focus upon a sufficiently broad and detailed conception of human goods is essential to the doctrine and is not the object of my concern. Rather, what is worthy of critical attention is the tendency amongst some (particularly in the developed, affluent part of the globe) to demand the provision of services and goods which are not prerequisite to the enjoyment of any particular right. This raises the question of what the benchmark or necessary threshold of any and all human rights must be. Put simply, we need to distinguish between genuine human rights and social privileges, for if too many of the latter are conceived of as the former then the ability of human rights to realise its ambition will be even more severely undermined.

Attempts to identify both what should be included as a human right and what the scope of any accepted human right may legitimately be are complicated by a number of factors. These factors may be classified as philosophical and political. Thus, any attempt to discern the threshold of the scope of human rights must engage with the philosophical question of what one must have access to in order to be human in the first place. The Universal Declaration of Human Rights identifies the purpose of human rights to be the protection and promotion of human dignity and the ability of all human beings to live a free and equal existence. While these are laudable commitments, identifying and specifying what they actually mean and entail is a very much more complicated task. This task is further confronted by the deeply problematic issue of the inherent normativity of the vision of humankind which the doctrine of human rights draws upon. A human rights-based definition of what it means to be human is not properly understood as a descriptive or empirical exercise. One might claim that a constitutive property of being human is the possession of a physical body and a functioning cerebral cortex. It is quite something else to claim that being human is possessing an inherent dignity or necessarily standing in a relation of moral equality with every other such physical entity. These should be understood not as purported descriptions of the human condition, as proposed visions of what is conducive to human wellbeing. As such, this approach cannot escape the web of normativity and morality. Human rights theory characteristically does not rest upon a description of the human condition. Rather, it offers a prescriptive vision of a morally desirable human condition. Against the arguments presented by, most notably Alan Gewirth, who seek to inscribe human rights as necessary attributes of human agency *per se*, it is far more accurate to conceive of human rights in terms which acknowledge the partiality and specificity of the account of the human condition which they aim to secure. This means that our understanding of the basis and scope of human rights should not be sought in 'nature' or by appeal to purportedly constitutively material attributes of humankind. Some will be reluctant to accept my argument that determining the basis and scope of human rights is an ineliminably normative exercise. For some this entails the denial of the possibility of defending human rights by appeal to epistemological certainties. It might also, thereby, be understood as exposing the doctrine to the apparently arbitrary and random intellectual terrain of post-modernism and moral relativism. On this view, human rights may no longer be understood as a *grand narrative* of humanity (to draw upon Jean-François Lyotard's (1979) terminology) but as merely one of a number of competing moral doctrines. This in turn is liable to be conceived of as exposing human rights to the vagaries of politics. If human rights can no longer be understood as resting upon sure and indubitable moral foundations then we are bound to accept their inherent contingency. The securing of the appeal and authority of the doctrine should no longer be pursued through moral argumentation but must be oriented instead towards the political process (Ignatieff, 2001). The legitimacy of human rights becomes thereby increasingly a measure of how successful human rights' supporters are in expounding the doctrine: the more people adhere to the doctrine the greater its political legitimacy will be.

Resorting to politics as a consequence of a loss of faith in human rights foundations has become an established tactic amongst some within the human rights community. However, while a politically strategic approach to human rights campaigning is to be encouraged, embracing a fully political account of the basis and scope of doctrine contains a number of potential dangers for identifying and defending a reasonable threshold for the enjoyment of human rights. Most obviously, if one's defence of human rights becomes entwined with how many people approve of and support the doctrine, the doctrine itself will be vulnerable to populations and circumstances which are not supportive of its claims and aspirations. This might take the form of a political élite which has successfully manipulated popular opinion into adopting a critical outlook upon human rights. Thus, a commitment to fundamental human rights might be represented as the attempted continuation of western imperialism amongst those whose independence from former colonial rule must exclude embracing their former coloniser's hypocritical values and ideals. Alternatively, a commitment to human rights might be presented as entailing a rejection of the authority of the divine being and sacred texts the strictures of which extend beyond places of religious worship to influence the design and actions of public and governmental authorities. Finally, human rights might be conceived of as a means by which unpopular minorities may continue to be shielded from the (majority) will of the people. Human rights are not only politically contro-versial in 'non-western', undemocratic societies, after all. Indeed, the opposite issue may also arise, particularly within the more affluent and developed soci-eties. Thus, if human rights are to be understood as ultimately reducible to political action and factors, it is perfectly conceivable that the scope of any given human right may be extended as a consequence of the success of a particular constituency in demanding and pursuing this outcome. Where human rights are systematically abused such an outcome is obviously to be welcomed. However, in circumstances of relative prosperity, for example, inflating the necessary provision of some right or other will (in zero-sum game circumstances) adversely affect the status and scope of other rights. The politi-cisation of human rights raises the very real risk of a fragmentation of the doctrine into competing constituencies concerned to promote the rights which particularly concern them, but the achievement of which may have adverse consequences for the rights of others, not just within the same political community but also, and more profoundly, for those other members of the global human community who do not possess the same passport.

Human rights theory must itself be contextualised. The doctrine is simulta-neously a response to and a consequence of a broader attempt to establish a genuinely authoritative and global morality. Many obstacles confront this ambition. Some concern the philosophical difficulty of formulating any moral theory capable of encompassing all of humanity. Others are more overtly material or practical in character, and concern the extent to which human beings are fundamentally separated from each other by political boundaries and the distribution of wealth and resources, to name just two. A sufficiently deep and broad commitment to human rights cannot be achieved by appeals to their alleged self-evidently true nature or to largely empty rhetoric. In many parts of the world, wholesale populations are systematically denied their fundamental rights, whilst in others demands are made in the name of human rights for services and goods which call into question our understanding of the legitimate scope of human rights. What is required is the identification of a threshold criterion which acknowledges its inherently normative character, appeals nevertheless to criteria which are not unduly controversial and, finally, encompasses recognition that a commitment to human rights entails a commit-ment to a broadly cosmopolitan account of the moral community. To this end, I have argued for a 'back to basics' type of approach, which views human rights as, first and foremost, motivated by a systematic attempt to secure all human beings from the threat of and exposure to all forms of systematic and significant human suffering. Human life cannot be devoid of suffering. We are, ultimately, embodied beings with a finite existence. Unlike (perhaps) most, if not all, other such beings we human beings are blessed and cursed with the capacity imaginatively to transcend our circumstances; to conceive of ourselves as other than we are. We are thereby exposed to two different forms of suffering: the physiological deprivation of our fundamental needs and a psychological frustration which results from the dissonance between what we are and what we aim to become. Both of these are inherent features of the human condition, and human rights must embrace both. However, the latter form of suffering introduces an indeterminacy to any attempt to secure the conditions for overcoming and preventing systematic human suffering. An artist may suffer because her work goes unappreciated. A lover may suffer because his love is unreciprocated. Parents may suffer because their children have opted for alternative values and ideals. None of these, however, can be considered human rights violations. They refer to phenomena which are not included within the human rights framework or they inflate the proper appli-cation of a recognised human right. Human rights must aim to eradicate systematic physiological suffering in the many forms it takes. Human rights must also aim to provide protection to individuals from those systematic forms of psychological suffering which, for example, oppress people for their beliefs and conscience, or exclude the possibility of developing ideals and values which are not approved of by those in power. However, they must not be extended to cover more overtly partial attempts to secure for particular constituencies the satisfaction of wants the realisation of which amounts to a mere social privilege. What constitutes suffering remains, admittedly, a controversial area of concern and debate. Any appeal to suffering as the ground for human rights must remain cognisant of those factors which prevent any easy or rudimentary account of the basis and scope of human rights. Social and cultural factors are obviously deeply influential upon how human suffering is identified and measured. Similarly, a concern to prevent suffering may run the risk of resorting to an unduly paternalist approach to regulating human affairs, which compounds the problem by thwarting some people's expressed will and commitments. These are all factors which require a much closer analysis if my argument is to stand upon sufficiently robust foundations.

Despite the undoubtedly complex and incomplete vision of an appeal to the prevention of suffering as the principal ground for human rights, I positively advocate it as a means of defining the scope of human rights within an increasingly interdependent world. My approach has been significantly influenced by James Nickel's (1987) attempt to determine the basis and scope of human rights. As I discussed in Chapter 1, Nickel proposes the standard of the conditions for a minimally good life as the ground upon which human rights may legitimately rest. I have sought to amend Nickel's approach and to argue, in effect, that the conditions for a minimally good life should be understood, at least at the present time, as being free from the threat and effects of systematic and significant suffering. Some will, no doubt, view this approach as unnecessarily modest and lacking in ambition. My approach, unlike that of say Alan Gewirth, appears to ask relatively little of human rights. Against this, I argue that we have to think and act from where we currently are and not from the unduly idealised terrain which some human rights advocates tend to occupy. 'We' must also be clear about who 'we' are in this context. A commitment to human rights entails an obligation to think and act from a broadly cosmopolitan standpoint. Seen from the perspective of a global moral human community, what might appear to be a modest ambition of overcoming systematic and significant suffering to some remains an unrealised aspiration for many. This, ostensibly modest, ambition is actually profoundly radical and demanding for a world in which so many are continually denied the prospect of an existence free from long-standing and far-reaching suffering. The elimination of such forms of suffering should be the first and most immediate goal of the human rights community for this new millennium. If and once this is achieved, then and only then may we extend our ambition and our criteria for the purpose of human rights.

UNIVERSALITY FOR ALL

The insistence that human rights are valid for all human beings everywhere logically entails a commitment to the universality principle. The very fact that countless millions of human beings do not enjoy an existence free from systematic and significant human suffering amounts to a flagrant violation of the universality principle and provides a fundamental motive for seeking to have these people's human rights adequately secured. However, in recent years the universality principle has attracted consistent criticism from some who, nevertheless, remain committed to the human rights cause. Typically these critics originate from and identify with what might be loosely defined as the 'non-western' world, as exemplified by the likes of the African Makau Mutua and the Palestinian Edward Said. Thinkers such as these have sought to expose and criticise 'western' hypocrisy in respect of both the theory and the practice of human rights. All too often, visions and formulations of what might be substantively universal can be shown more accurately to reflect unduly partial and specific perspectives and experiences. All too often, western moral and political conceptions have been simply assumed to be necessarily universal: moral validity is thereby reduced to a function of political and economic hegemony. On this view, the history of humanity's development is necessarily reflexive of the western experience (Fukuyama, 1989). This is further compounded by western political élites' failure to comply with their own professed standards in their relations with the non-western world. A commitment to human rights becomes a commitment to the values and ideals of a specific section of humankind which are then subsequently employed or set aside depending upon how well they serve or cohere with the specific policy goals of powerful nations such as the United States or members of the European Union.

Some non-western critics have gone so far as to associate western values and all appeals to human rights as ultimately hypocritical and morally defunct attempts to perpetuate colonialism in a less direct way (Shivji, 1989). However, this goes too far in the opposite direction in its implicit idealisation of purportedly indigenous traditions and practices which may themselves have been based upon systematic human rights abuses. If some attempts to defend the universality of human rights have been unduly Eurocentric in their assumption that the rest of humankind ought to or does share the values and ideals associated most closely with the West and others have thrown the baby of human rights out with the bath-water of Eurocentricity, what seems to be required is an account of universality which emanates from and extends to cover many, if not all, of humankind's commitments.

I argued in Chapter 3 against the view which holds that the universal validity of human rights may ultimately be traced back to their preceding any given social or political configurations and conditions. This view of human rights as natural rights obscures from view the very sociality of human rights, and simply ignores the extent to which the existence and maintenance of human rights require an established set of material conditions. This is not to imply that human rights are therefore mere social determinations, nor to claim that human rights have purchase only in those communities which acknowledge them. Human rights appeal to an existential condition which, I have argued, all human beings have an interest in securing for themselves and (ultimately) for others too. While this condition is subject to and influenced by differing social perspectives and experiences, no single and specific community or society has a monopoly upon how it is conceived of. If human rights are to remain appealing to a diverse range of human communities they must be capable of addressing each of those communities in terms which are sufficiently familiar and compelling. This may require, in certain circumstances, a reappraisal of how some human rights have been conventionally conceived. An obvious example can be found in the difficulties many human rights advocates have experienced when confronted by overtly collectivist human communities, which genuinely do not share the always somewhat idealised estimation of the morally sovereign individual which figures so prominently in human rights jurisprudence. Granting collective rights to endangered indigenous communities as a means to protect their land, their language or their customs has proven to be a deeply controversial issue. Part of this controversy lies in the refusal or inability of some to accept the possible legitimacy of alternative ways of living and alternative ways of conceiving of what may possess moral value in the first place. As a general principle, one may argue that, all other things being equal, if an established cultural practice is deemed to be incompatible with some existing understanding or application of a specific human right, then we should seek to revise the human right better to cohere with the practice, rather than insist that the practice stop as a condition of receiving the validation and support of the human rights community. This does not amount to a capitulation to moral relativism. That an alternative to conventional western approaches to human rights is likely to be greeted as such is evidence of just how great a hold such partial perspectives have enjoyed over human rights. My argument also does not intend unconditionally to validate whatever the powerful members of any community insist should be the case. A commitment to human rights entails the drawing of a line in the metaphorical sand. A commitment to human rights also entails adopting a stance of critical independence from what may be generally accepted to be true and valid. Identifying where one draws the line and how one may remain engaged with but not ultimately assimilated by a given social reality requires an appeal to the kind of common existential ground I identify with being free from systematic and significant suffering. An account of human rights based upon an understanding of universality for all urgently requires the development of an approach which encompasses the complexity of the human condition.

REALISING HUMAN RIGHTS

I have argued against the complacency of those views which assert that the normative aim of securing general or unanimous support for human rights has been achieved. The extent to which so many human beings continue to languish in conditions which frustrate and deny their fundamental rights indicates not just a continuing practical and institutional failure, but also the limits of the normative commitment to human rights. A reasonable test of a normative commitment towards, for example, alleviating human suffering is the extent to which this commitment proves to be genuinely action-guiding. On this test, the commitment to human rights remains partial, at best. In the preceding two sections of this chapter I argued for a particular understanding of what human rights should aim to secure and for whom. This section focuses upon the means for pursuing those ends.

A commitment to protect and promote human rights is necessarily addressed to all human beings as such. Human rights is a thoroughly and necessarily cosmopolitan doctrine. However, cosmopolitan ethics are confronted by a number of empirical obstacles which are all too familiar. The principal institutional entity in the current global political system remains the sovereign nation-state. Individual nation-states are also principally legally responsible for protecting their citizens' human rights. Unfortunately, many states are more prone to act as poachers rather than game-keepers when it comes to regulating the field of human rights. The principal entity responsible for human rights is also the foremost violator of human rights. The reasons why states violate human rights are complex and multi-faceted. It would be wrong to view such violations as always resulting from the evil doings of evil men. Some human rights abuses fit this particular bill, undoubtedly, but many others do not. In these instances, policies directed towards violating human rights may appear to be more consistent with the broader national interest of the state in question. The ability of other states to intervene in such affairs is limited by international legal factors, such as the UN Charter and calculations of political and economic interests. Ultimately, an appeal to national sovereignty provides one of the principal mechanisms for perpetrating human rights abuses and a lack of sufficient will to confront such abuses. In the face of a well-established and deeply embedded geo-political structure, mere rhetorical appeals to a global family or humankind will prove to be largely useless. While it may seem veritably blasphemous to some, I think we must acknowledge that the sovereign nation-state retains a significant degree of power and influence. Rather than dismissing the state as inherently hostile to human rights, we require a more nuanced appreciation of existing legal realities in respect of the state's role as the front-line human rights duty-bearer. Seen from this perspective, the task becomes one of exerting pressures upon states to uphold, rather than violate, human rights. In any specific and given instance this will require an intimate understanding of the history and contemporary circumstances of the state and society in question. It will also require facilitating internal constituencies in their pursuit of their own human rights.

External campaigns must not and will not prove able simply to substitute for the lack of a sufficiently established domestic constituency for human rights. This task ought to fall upon a number of different external agents: states, inter-governmental agencies, civil society and non-governmental organisations, and finally private individuals whose stated abhorrence of human rights violating regimes should be encouraged by some form of support for attempts to over-come these conditions. The principal aim and challenge of any such concerted campaign should be to persuade sovereign nation-states that they do, indeed, have a fundamental interest in securing the fundamental human rights of all of their citizens and, beyond this, in contributing to campaigns to achieve the same end for those states lacking the will or the means to do likewise.

An appeal to national interest is fraught with many significant problems and obstacles. No one should ever imagine that genuinely realising the ambi-tion of human rights will prove to be particularly easy. Arguably, one of the foremost obstacles concerns who represents, or speaks for, the state. We currently inhabit a world of notional democracies. After the fall of state social-ism a motley collection of newly independent states declared themselves to be 'democratic'. In many cases, these claims do not extend beyond the mere impressions of words upon constitutions which power-holders almost entirely ignore. What democracy must consist of remains open to debate within the realms of political theory and constitutional law. Human rights have made an important contribution to our understanding of what democracy ought to secure. From a human rights-based perspective, democracy does not refer to what the majority desires, *per se*. Nor is democracy the means by which estab-lished political élites secure some nominal legitimacy every few years for their continuing dominance and control. A commitment to human rights serves to limit the exercise of power and to direct legitimate government towards secur-ing the protection and promotion of each and every citizen's fundamental human rights. A commitment to human rights must necessarily entail a commitment to according an equal legal and moral standing to each and every citizen, including those who may belong to or be identified with communities or constituencies that are unpopular with the majority of the electorate or consistently critical of elected governments. In this context, a commitment to human rights might well appear to be contrary to or antithetical to the narrower but more immediate interests of those who wield power and those who voted for them. Herein lies one of the greatest challenges for the protection and promotion of human rights. To claim that human rights have secured a norma-tive hegemony in the contemporary world is to imply that campaigns to protect and promote human rights will, all other things being equal, be neces-sarily popular. This is patently false. In many demonstrable incidences within the developed and the developing world, attempts to promote human rights have proven to be unpopular amongst those who, rightly or wrongly, perceive a commitment to human rights as enhancing someone else's welfare or well-being at the expense of their own. In these situations, a commitment to human rights has typically been perceived as diminishing the capital (broadly defined) of those who have become accustomed to the status quo. It would be a mistake simply to dismiss such positions out of hand. While many of us might be inclined to describe them as manifestations of unenlightened interest or the bogus attempts of the privileged to legitimise inequality and unfairness, an effective campaign for human rights as a necessary element of a genuinely democratic system must effectively engage with and address such sentiments.

I argued earlier against the view that human rights are essential attributes of human agency *per se*. One might similarly argue against a view which held that a commitment to securing human rights-respecting democracies requires demonstrating to all concerned that their interests will be best served by promoting human rights over the pursuit of more partial political interests. It is, if you will, philosophically naïve to assume that all political agents necessarily share a fundamental interest in human rights. Political despots and those whose continuing privilege depends upon their association with human rights-abusing regimes do not have a fundamental interest in the substitution of their rule with one which is founded upon a respect for human rights. The transformation of notional democracies or overtly authoritarian regimes into human rights-respecting democracies will result in winners and losers. The gains of the winners, needless to say, will far outweigh the losses of the losers. This may look like an unduly utilitarian argument to some. As such, it may even be dismissed as ultimately incompatible with a commitment to the true spirit of human rights. While my argument is motivated by a concern for greater political realism, so to speak, it does not require or sanction any subsequent violation of human rights' commitment to equality. It would not extend to sanctioning the victorious 'human rights party' in turn violating the fundamental rights of those who have lost their power. The sovereign nation-state remains an entity the power and resources of which ought to be directed towards promoting human rights. As a very general directive, campaigns to achieve this end should be directed towards promoting and supporting domestic constituencies' attempts to secure their own human rights. This, in turn, ought to be pursued through the development of genuinely democratic conditions. A commitment to human rights entails a commitment to an account of democracy which is bound by a prior principle of fundamental respect for the equality of all citizens. This approach stands opposed to an alternative and well-established view of democracy as the means by which the majority may express and seek to secure their own partial interests. Typically, the losers within such a system count the cost in diminished human rights. From the perspective of human rights this is manifestly intolerable. The task which confronts domestic and international supporters of human rights in this regard is to seek to create democratic systems and institutions of which a commitment to human rights is an integral component. This very formidable task will require not just exercises in institutional reform but also campaigns to raise individuals' consciousness. Not everyone has a legitimate interest in overcoming human rights-abusing regimes. Nevertheless, the vast majority do have such an interest. If and once these conditions are achieved, an interest in maintaining human rights will continue, so that being on the losing side of a free and fair election will not thereby jeopardise anyone's human rights. Human rights function as a veritable insurance policy in this regard.

I have proposed that the basis for our commitment to human rights as a legitimate moral doctrine should begin with a concern for systematic and significant suffering. Needless to say, further theorising and argument are required adequately to support this proposal. For the moment, however, it is important not to misconstrue my application of this proposal. On the face of it, some might draw the conclusion that a focus on suffering will serve to prioritise economic, social and cultural rights over their civil and political counterparts. On this view, physiological and material suffering might be thought of as somehow more tangible and immediate than the more participatory rights found within the civil and political domain: that the avoidance of starvation is more urgent and important than ensuring a fair trial or freedom of expression. However, I have also argued in favour of Shue's notion of rights holism. In effect, a holistic account of human rights calls for a more nuanced understanding of human wellbeing and its counterpart: suffering. Human beings suffer as a consequence of having opportunities to lead a minimally good life systematically denied them. Being denied an opportunity to participate in the affairs of the political community to which they are subject will often increase the likelihood of these same individuals being denied access to the basic material 'nutrients' of an adequate social existence. If we wish to realise the ambition of human rights, then we should hesitate before reinforcing the unduly artificial and often damaging distinction between the two principal categories of human rights.

Achieving the ambition of human rights will require more than mere proclamations of the doctrine's alleged hegemonic status. It is also going to require more than simply assuming that the responsibility for achieving this task must necessarily and exclusively fall upon some specialised agency or political institution. I have argued that a genuinely democratic state has a thoroughly constructive contribution to make to the protection of human rights. I have also argued that the realm of this protection must extend to include human rights as an integral phenomenon, which encompasses the necessities for leading a life free from the threat or effects of significant and systematic suffering. I have also argued for the importance of orienting human rights' promotion towards facilitating and empowering domestic constituencies in their pursuit of their human rights, thereby reducing the prospect of human rights being viewed as some culturally alien imposition by privileged (and sometimes hypocritical) outsiders. A crucial element for realising these ambitions concerns the notion of duty to others and the extent to which human beings are willing and able to act in support of a substantively minimal global ethic. If human rights are to be more effectively protected in the coming years then private individuals will need to be persuaded that they too bear human rights responsibilities, as correlates of their possession of human rights. This is most urgent in the case of the unequal distribution of global wealth and resources. Even during times of economic 'downturn' the wealth of the affluent peoples of the globe is directly related to the poverty of our languishing counterparts. In the face of global economic forces and the huge sums of wealth involved, even conscientious individuals are liable to conclude that there is nothing that they can do about it. A commitment to human rights entails a commitment to the view that all human beings, ultimately, occupy a single moral space and community. The design and practices of institutions ultimately serve to obscure and frustrate this realisation. However, a commitment to human rights entails a refusal to accept that human suffering is somehow inevitable and insuperable. The human rights 'community' needs to encourage the view that all of the variables of human identity (regional, national, religious, ethnic, gender, able-bodiedness and age) are undeniably relevant to questions of the appropriate means for pursuing human rights, but are ultimately irrelevant to the ends of human rights. Likewise, the need to encourage a view of shared membership of a single and global moral community needs to diminish a perceived professionalisation of human rights work, which posits human rights to be a specialised preserve of a small group of highly trained professionals. The work of such people remains indispensable and will always be a necessary component of the human rights project, but it should never be seen as thereby sufficient. As a duty, a commitment to human rights falls upon us all, and especially those who have come to take our human rights for granted while others' human rights are consistently abused. The realisation of human rights will require a vast diffusion of a concern for human rights among those populations which are not daily presented with the threat of significant and systematic human suffering.

CONCLUSION

Beyond the more overt motive of academic advancement, I have written this book in an attempt to confront and analyse a number of demonstrable myths and misunderstandings concerning the basis, scope and character of human rights. In so doing, I have also sought to develop an alternative account of human rights. This account is motivated by both a commitment to human rights as a global moral doctrine and a recognition of the obstacles which confront their satisfactory realisation. Conceived of in the relatively minimal terms which I propose, human rights offer hope and guidance in a world still beset by intolerable suffering. Their very existence also confounds those who would argue that human history has always been and always will be a slaughter-bench. I acknowledge that my arguments remain incomplete and in need of further development. However, if I have successfully caused the reader to think again about human rights then part of the task will have been achieved. If, in addition, I have encouraged the reader to engage more extensively in the analysis and practice of human rights in a manner which recognises that the precarious status of human rights demands an urgent commitment to better understanding and realising them, then my aspiration for this work will have been fully realised. Human rights challenge us all to be more humane towards one another. Let us hope it is a challenge that humankind is capable of meeting.

References

Anderson, Benedict (1983) *Imagined Communities: Reflections on the Origin and spread of Nationalism* (London: Verso).

Anderson-Gold, Sharon (2001) *Cosmopolitanism and Human Rights* (Cardiff: University of Wales Press).

An-Na'im, A. (1991) *Toward an Islamic Reformation: Civil Liberties, Human Rights and International Law* (Syracuse: Syracuse University Press).

An-Na'im, A. (ed.) (1992) *Human Rights in Cross-Cultural Perspectives: a Quest for Consensus* (Philadelphia, Penn: University of Philadelphia Press).

Aquinas, Thomas (1981) *Summa theologica/St. Thomas Aquinas* (trans. Fathers of the English Dominican Province, Westminster, Md: Christian Classics).

Arrow, Kenneth (1963) *Social Choices and Individual Values* (2nd edition, New York: Wiley).

Barry, Brian (1991) 'Can States be Moral? International Morality & the Compliance Problem', in B. Barry, *Liberty and Justice: Essays in Political Theory* (New York: Oxford University Press) Vol. 2, pp. 159–81.

Barry, Brian (2001) *Culture and Equality: an Egalitarian Critique of Multiculturalism* (Cambridge, Mass: Harvard University Press).

Becker, Gary (2000) *Social Economics: Market Behaviour in a Social Environment* (Cambridge, Mass: Belknap Press).

Beetham, David (1999) *Democracy and Human Rights* (Cambridge: Polity).

Beitz, Charles (1999) *Political Theory and International Relations* (Princeton, NJ: Princeton University Press).

Benedict, Ruth (1935) *Patterns of Culture* (London: Routledge).

Bentham, Jeremy (1987) *Principles of Morals and Legislation* (London: Methuen).

Berlin, Isaiah (1969) 'Two Concepts of Liberty', in I. Berlin, *Four Essays on Liberty* (Oxford: Oxford University Press), pp. 118–72.

Bielefeldt, Heiner (2000) '"Western" Versus "Islamic" Human Rights Conceptions? A Critique of Cultural Essentialism in the Discussion of Human Rights', 28(1), *Political Theory*, 90–121.

Bhagwati, Jadish (2000) *The Wind of a Hundred Days: How Washington Mismanaged Globalisation* (Cambridge, Mass: MIT Press).

Blumenberg, Hans (1983) *The Legitimacy of the Modern Age* (trans. Robert M. Wallace) (Cambridge, Mass: MIT Press).

Bradley, F.H. (1999) *Ethical Studies* (London: Routledge/Thoemmes).

Campbell, Tom (2006) *Rights: a Critical Introduction* (London: Routledge).

Caney, Simon (2005) *Justice Beyond Borders* (Oxford: Oxford University Press).

Chan, J. (1999) 'A Confucian Perspective on Human Rights for Contemporary China', in J.A. Bauer and D.A. Bell (eds.) *The East Asian Challenge for Human Rights* (Cambridge: Cambridge University Press), pp. 212–37.

Cohen, G.A. (1978) *Marx's Theory of History: a Defence* (Oxford: Clarendon Press).

Connolly, William E. (1993) *The Terms of Political Discourse* (3rd edition, Oxford: Blackwell).

Cranston, Maurice (1973) *What are Human Rights?* (London: Bodley Head).

Cranston, Maurice (1991) *The Noble Savage: Jean-Jacques Rousseau, 1754–1762* (London: Allen Lane).

Donnelly, Jack (1985) 'Cultural Relativism and Universal Human Rights' 6(4) *Human Rights Quarterly,* 400–419.

Donnelly, Jack (1998) *International Human Rights* (Boulder, Co: Westview Press).

Donnelly, Jack (1999) 'Human Rights and Asian Values: A Defence of "Western" Universalism', in J.A. Bauer and D.A. Bell (eds.) *The East Asian Challenge for Human Rights* (Cambridge: Cambridge University Press), pp. 60–87.

Donnelly, Jack (2002) *Universal Rights in Theory and Practice* (Ithaca, NY: Cornell University Press).

Dundes Renteln, Alison (1988) 'Relativism and the Search for Human Rights' 90(1) *American Anthropologist,* 56–72.

Dworkin, Ronald (1986) *Law's Empire* (Cambridge, Mass: Belknap Press).

Dworkin, Ronald (1990) 'Rights as Trumps' in Jeremy Waldron (ed.) *Theories of Rights* (Oxford: Oxford University Press), pp. 153–67.

Dworkin, Ronald (1996) *Freedom's Law: the Moral Reading of the American Constitution* (Cambridge, Mass: Harvard University Press).

Elster, Jon (1993) 'Majority Rule and Individual Rights', in S. Shute and S. Hurley (eds.) *On Human Rights: The Oxford Amnesty Lectures 1993* (New York: Basic Books), pp. 175–216.

Fagan, Andrew (2006) 'Challenging the Right of Exit Remedy in the Political Theory of Cultural Diversity', 7(1) *Essays in Philosophy,* Jan. 2006, 185–214.

Fagan, Andrew (2006b) 'Buying Right: Consuming Ethically and Human Rights' in Janet Dine and Andrew Fagan (eds.) *Human Rights and Capitalism: a Multidisciplinary Perspective on Globalisation* (Cheltenham: Edward Elgar), pp. 115–144.

Fagan, Andrew (2008) 'Back to Basics: Human Rights and the Suffering

Imperative' 5(1) *Essex Human Rights Review: 25th Anniversary Special Edition* (July 2008), 91–96.

Feinberg, Joel (1980) *Rights, Justice and the Bounds of Liberty: Essays in Social Philosophy* (Princeton, NJ: Princeton University Press).

Finnis, John (1980) *Natural Law & Natural Rights* (Oxford: Clarendon Press).

Freeman, Michael (1995) 'Are There Collective Rights?' 43 *Political Studies* 25–40.

Freeman, Michael (2002) *Human Rights: an Interdisciplinary Approach* (Oxford: Polity).

Fukuyama, Francis (1989) 'The End of History?' 16 *The National Interest* 3–18.

Gauthier, David (1986) *Morals by Agreement* (Oxford: Clarendon Press).

George, Susan (1988) *A Fate Worse Than Debt* (Harmondsworth: Penguin).

George, Susan (1992) *The Debt Boomerang: How Third World Debt Harms Us All* (London: Pluto).

Gewirth, Alan (1982) *Human Rights: Essays on Justification and Applications* (Chicago: Chicago University Press).

Gewirth, Alan (1996) *The Community of Rights* (Chicago: Chicago University Press).

Gutmann, Amy and Dennis Thompson (1996) *Democracy and Disagreement* (Cambridge, Mass.: Belknap Press).

Hart, H.L.A. (1994) *The Concept of Law* (Oxford: Clarendon Press).

Hayek, F. (1960) *The Constitution of Liberty* (London: Routledge & Kegan Paul).

Held, David (2006) *Models of Democracy* (3rd edition, Cambridge: Polity).

Henkin, Louis (1990) *The Age of Rights* (New York: Columbia University Press).

Hobbes, Thomas (1985) *Leviathan* (Harmondsworth: Penguin).

Hohfeld, Wesley (1978) *Fundamental Legal Conceptions as Applied in Judicial Reasoning* (Westport, Conn.: Greenwood Press).

Horkheimer, Max and Theodor Adorno (1973) *Dialectic of Enlightenment* (trans. John Cumming, London: Verso).

Howard, Rhoda (1986) *Human Rights in Commonwealth Africa* (Totowa, N.J.: Rowman & Littlefield).

Hume, David (1975) *Enquiries Concerning Human Understanding and Concerning the Principles of Morals* (Oxford: Clarendon Press).

Hunt, Paul (1996) *Reclaiming Social Rights: International and Comparative Perspectives* (Aldershot: Dartmouth).

Huntington, Samuel (1996) *The Clash of Civilizations and the Remaking of World Order* (New York: Simon & Schuster).

Ignatieff, Michael (2001) *Human Rights as Politics and Idolatry* (Princeton, N.J. : Princeton University Press).

Ishay, Micheline (2004) *The History of Human Rights: From Ancient Times to the Globalization Era* (Berkeley, Cal.: University of California Press).

Jones, Peter (1994) *Rights* (Basingstoke: Macmillan).

Kant, Immanuel (1964) *The Groundwork for the Metaphysic of Morals* (trans. H.J. Paton, New York: Harper Torchbooks).

Kant, Immanuel (1993) *Critique of Practical Reason* (trans. Lewis White Beck, 3rd edition, New York: Macmillan).

Keenan, George F. (1964) 'Morality and Foreign Policy', 64(2) *Foreign Affairs*, 205–18.

Kelsen, Hans (1978) *The Pure Theory of Law* (trans. Max Knight, Berkeley, Cal.: University of California Press).

Kukathas, Chandran (2003) *The Liberal Archipelago: A Theory of Diversity & Freedom* (Oxford: Oxford University Press).

Kukathas, C. and P. Pettit (1990) *Rawls: A Theory of Justice and Its Critics* (Cambridge: Polity).

Kymlicka, Will (1989) *Liberalism, Community and Culture* (Oxford: Clarendon Press).

Kymlicka, Will (1992) 'The Rights of Minority Cultures. Reply to Kukathas', 20(1) *Political Theory,* 140–46.

Kymlicka, Will (1995) *Multicultural Citizenship: a Liberal Theory of Group Rights* (Oxford: Clarendon Press).

Locke, John (1988) *Two Treatises of Government* (Cambridge: Cambridge University Press).

Luttwak, Edward (1999) *Turbo Capitalism: Winners and Losers in the Global Economy* (London: Orion).

Lyotard, Jean-François (1979) *La Condition Postmoderne: rapport sur la savoir* (Paris: Editions Minuit).

MacIntyre, Alasdair (1984) *After Virtue: a Study in Moral Theory* (2nd edition, Notre Dame, Ind.: University of Notre Dame Press).

MacIntyre, Alasdair (1988) *Whose Justice? Which Rationality?* (Notre Dame, Ind.: University of Notre Dame Press).

Mackie, J.L. (1977) *Ethics: Inventing Right & Wrong* (Harmondsworth: Penguin).

Marx, Karl (1978) *Capital, Vol. 1,* in R.C. Tucker (ed.) *The Marx-Engels Reader* (2nd edition, New York & London: W.W. Norton and Co.), pp. 294–438.

McGoldrick, Dominic (2006) *Human Rights and Religion: the Islamic Headscarf Debate in Europe* (Oxford: Hart).

Mendus, Susan (ed.) (1988) *Justifying Toleration: Conceptual and Historical Perspectives* (Cambridge: Cambridge University Press).

Mernissi, Fatima (1991) *Women and Islam: an Historical and Theological Enquiry* (trans. by Mary Jo Lakeland, Oxford: Blackwell).

Miller, David (1995) *On Nationality* (New York: Clarendon Press).

Miller, David (2000) 'National Self-Determination and Global Justice', in D. Miller, *Citizenship and National Identity* (Cambridge: Polity), pp. 161–79.

Morgenthau, Hans (1951) *In Defense of the National Interest: A Critical Examination of US Foreign Policy* (New York: Knopf).

Mulhall, Stephen and Adam Swift, (1992) *Liberals and Communitarians* (Oxford: Blackwell).

Mullerson, Rein (1997) *Human Rights Diplomacy* (London: Routledge).

Mutua, Makau (2002) *Human Rights: a Political and Cultural Critique* (Philadelphia, Penn.: University of Pennsylvania Press).

Nagel, Thomas (1986) *The View From Nowhere* (New York: Oxford University Press).

Nickel, James (1987) *Making Sense of Human Rights: Philosophical Reflections on the Universal Declaration of Human Rights* (Berkeley, Cal.: University of California Press).

Nietzsche, Friedrich (1967) *On the Genealogy of Morals* (trans. Walter Kaufmann and R.J. Hollingdale, New York: Vintage Books).

Nozick, Robert (1974) *Anarchy, State and Utopia* (Oxford: Blackwell).

Nussbaum, Martha (2002) *Women and Human Development: the Capabilities Approach* (Cambridge: Cambridge University Press).

Okin, Susan Moller (1999) *Is Multiculturalism Bad for Women?* (Princeton, N.J.: Princeton University Press).

Orend, Brian (2002) *Human Rights: Concept and Context* (Peterborough, Ont.: Broadview Press).

Othman, N. (1999) 'Grounding Human Rights Arguments in non-Western Culture: *Shari'a* and the Citizenship Rights of Women in a Modern Islamic State' in J.A. Bauer and D.A. Bell (eds.) *The East Asian Challenge for Human Rights* (Cambridge: Cambridge University Press), pp.169–92.

Parekh, Bhiku (2000) *Rethinking Multiculturalism: Cultural Diversity and Political Theory* (Basingstoke: Macmillan).

Patomaki, Heikki (2001) *Democratising Globalisation: the Leverage of the Tobin Tax* (London: Zed Books).

Paul, Ellen Frankel, Fred D. Miller, Jr., and Jeffrey Paul (eds.), (1994) *Cultural Pluralism and Moral Knowledge* (Cambridge: Cambridge University Press).

Pogge, Thomas (1992) 'Cosmopolitanism and Sovereignty', 44 *Ethics* 48–75.

Pogge, Thomas (2002) *World Poverty and Human Rights: Cosmopolitan Responsibilities and Reforms* (Malden, Mass.: Blackwell).

Pollis, A. and P. Schwab (2000) 'Human Rights: A Western Construct with Limited Applicability', in A. Pollis and P. Schwab, *Human Rights: New Perspectives, New Realities* (Boulder, Colo.: Lynne Rienner), pp. 1–18.

Rao, Arati (1991) 'Speaking/Seeking a Common Language: Women, the Hindu Right and Human Rights in India', in C. Gustafson and P. Juviler (eds.) *Religion and Human Rights* (Armonk: M.E. Sharpe), pp. 117–40.

160 *Human rights*

Rawls, John (1971) *Theory of Justice* (Cambridge, Mass.: Harvard University Press).

Rawls, John (1993) *Political Liberalism* (New York: Columbia University Press).

Rawls, John (1999) *The Law of Peoples* (Cambridge, Mass.: Harvard University Press).

Rorty, Richard (1993) 'Human Rights: Rationality and Sentimentality', in S. Shute and S. Hurley (eds.) *On Human Rights: the Oxford Amnesty Lectures* (New York: Basic Books), pp.111–34.

Rousseau, Jean-Jacques (1968) *The Social Contract* (trans. Maurice Cranston, London: Penguin).

Roxborough, Ian (1979) *Theories of Underdevelopment* (London: Macmillan).

Sachs, Jeffrey (2005) *The End of Poverty: How We Can Make it Happen in our Lifetime* (London: Penguin).

Said, Edward (1978) *Orientalism* (London: Routledge & Kegan Paul).

Saliyeh, Emile (2003) 'The Status of Human Rights in the Middle East: Prospects and Challenges', in D.P. Forsythe and P.C. McMahon (eds.) *Human Rights and Diversity* (Lincoln, Neb.: University of Nebraska Press), pp. 252–78.

Samson, Colin (2003) *A Way of Life That Does Not Exist: Canada and the Extinguishment of the Innu* (London: Verso).

Sandel, Michael (1982) *Liberalism and the Limits of Justice* (Cambridge: Cambridge University Press).

Sayre-McCord, Geoffrey (1988) *Essays on Moral Realism* (Ithaca, N.Y.: Cornell University Press).

Scheffler, Samuel (2001) *Boundaries and Allegiances: Problems of Justice and Responsibility in Liberal Thought* (Oxford: Oxford University Press).

Schumpeter, Joseph (1954) *Capitalism, Socialism and Democracy* (4th edition, London: Unwin University Books).

Sen, Amartya (1981) *Poverty and Famines: an Essay on Entitlement and Deprivation* (Oxford: Clarendon Press).

Sen, Amartya (1999a) 'Human Rights and Economic Achievements', in J.R. Bauer and D.A. Bell (eds.) *The East Asian Challenge for Human Rights* (Cambridge: Cambridge University Press), pp. 88–99.

Sen, Amartya (1999b) *Development as Freedom* (New York: Knopf).

Shachar, Ayelet (2001) *Multicultural Jurisdictions: Cultural Differences and Women's Rights* (Cambridge: Cambridge University Press).

Sharples, R.W. (1996) *Stoics, Epicureans and Sceptics: an Introduction to Hellenistic Philosophy* (London: Routledge).

Shivji, Issa J. (1989) *The Concept of Human Rights in Africa* (London: Codesria Book Series).

Short, Damien (2008) *Reconciliation and Colonial Power: Indigenous Rights in Australia* (Burlington, Verm.: Ashgate Press).

Shue, Henry (1996) *Basic Rights: Subsistence, Affluence, and U.S. Foreign Policy* (2nd edition, Princeton, N.J.: Princeton University Press).

Steiner, Hillel (1994) *An Essay on Rights* (Oxford: Basil Blackwell).

Stevenson, C.L. (1944) *Ethics and Language* (New Haven, Conn.: Yale University Press).

Taylor, Charles (1989) *Sources of the Self: the Making of Modern Identity* (Cambridge, Mass.: Harvard University Press).

Turner, Bryan (2002), 'Outline of a Theory of Human Rights', 2(93) *Sociology,* 489–512.

Waldron, Jeremy (1999) *The Dignity of Legislation* (Cambridge: Cambridge University Press).

Waltz, Kenneth (1979) *Theory of International Politics* (Reading, Mass.: Addison-Wesley Pub. Co.).

Walzer, Michael (1994) *Thick and Thin: Moral Argument at Home and Abroad* (Notre Dame, Ind.: University of Notre Dame Press).

Waters, M. (1996) 'Human Rights and the Universalisation of Interests: Towards a Social Constructionist Approach', 30(3) *Sociology*, 593–600.

Westbrook, David (2004) *City of Gold: an Apology for Global Capitalism in a Time of Discontent* (New York: Routledge).

Williams, Bernard (1985) *Ethics and the Limits of Philosophy* (London: Fontana).

Wolf, Susan (1982) 'Moral Saints', 69 *Journal of Philosophy,* 419–439.

Wong, David (1991) 'Relativism', in Peter Singer (ed.) *A Companion to Ethics* (Oxford: Blackwell), pp. 442–50.

Young, Iris Marion (1990) *Justice and the Politics of Difference* (Princeton, N.J.: Princeton University Press).

Index